THE LAST GOLDFISH

The Last Goldfish

A True Tale of Friendship

Anita Lahey

Biblioasis
Windsor, Ontario

FIRST EDITION

Library and Archives Canada Cataloguing in Publication
Title: The last goldfish : a true tale of friendship / by Anita Lahey.
Names: Lahey, Anita, author.
Identifiers: Canadiana (print) 20190236612 | Canadiana (ebook) 20190236620 |
    ISBN 9781771963435 (softcover) | ISBN 9781771963442 (ebook)
Subjects: LCSH: Lahey, Anita. | LCSH: Lahey, Anita—Friends and associates. |
    LCSH: Cancer—Patients—Canada—Biography. | LCSH: Female friendship—
    Canada. | LCSH: Best friends—Canada—Biography. | LCSH: Women
    journalists—Canada—Biography. | LCGFT: Autobiographies.
Classification: LCC RC265.6.L34 A3 2020 | DDC 362.19699/40092—dc23

Edited by Janice Zawerbny
Copy-edited by Linda Pruessen
Typeset and Designed by Ingrid Paulson

 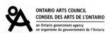

Published with the generous assistance of the Canada Council for the Arts,
which last year invested $153 million to bring the arts to Canadians
throughout the country, and the financial support of the Government
of Canada. Biblioasis also acknowledges the support of the Ontario Arts
Council (OAC), an agency of the Government of Ontario, which last year
funded 1,709 individual artists and 1,078 organizations in 204 communities
across Ontario, for a total of $52.1 million, and the contribution of the
Government of Ontario through the Ontario Book Publishing Tax Credit
and Ontario Creates.

PRINTED AND BOUND IN CANADA

For all my friends, near and far, especially
Monique, Rob M., and Trenna;

for Louisa's mother, father, and brothers, who so openly
welcomed me in my youth;

and for my own family, which did likewise for Louisa

CONTENTS

Some people are a country
and their deaths displace you.
Everything you shared with them
reminds you of it: part of you in exile
for the rest of your life.

—"Coming Through" by Bronwen Wallace
(*Common Magic*, 1985)

A Fish Story

IN EARLY GRADE NINE, I TEAMED UP WITH A GIRL NAMED Meredith for a science project. She was quiet and skittish, like a shy rabbit. We went to the pet store together and purchased six goldfish, six bowls, then divvied them up: three to her house, three to mine. Our plan was to place the fish in different environments—a busy kitchen, a dark closet, a bright windowsill—and try to gauge their contentment level by their behaviour. Which fish were more active, more hungry? The question, mine, had been whether a fish would prefer a darker home because it mimics the experience of a more natural habitat such as a lake.

But right away I found myself troubled by the idea of keeping fish captive. Watching my three fish swim circles in their bowls, I took notes, trying to describe their activity levels. I felt like a fraud. I had no idea how to assess the happiness of a fish, nor what kind of research to undertake to better inform our experiment. I hadn't the first clue how to penetrate the mysteries of the universe. And I couldn't explain any of this to Meredith. I'd roped her into this, so I put up a brave front when we sat down to compare results.

"How are *your* fish doing?" I asked.

She answered so softly I could barely hear. "One of them died." I stared. She was wringing her hands. "Do you think it was sick when we bought it?"

"It seemed like the other ones, didn't it?"

"I think so."

We sat in silence.

Suppose Meredith's fish had come home with me instead. Say the guy at the store had pulled a different specimen from the tank. The fish's bowl had been placed in a prime location, on the windowsill in Meredith's bedroom, south-facing. Maybe fish, like African violets, shrivelled in direct sunlight? I was overwhelmed by potential variables; I was *so* not ready for science. I was sure that none of our class-mates had a dead creature on their hands. But I also doubted any of them had taken this assignment so keenly to heart.

I'd picked Meredith for a partner because she didn't make me nervous. Maybe it made sense, now that I was out of the little elementary school with a graduating class of twenty-eight, to start aligning myself with more kids like me, who were into such things as books. But I was relieved when our experiment was finished, our results handed in. In the drawings for our report, Meredith had attempted to depict the dead fish, floating in its bowl. It looked like a tiny piece of driftwood.

In French class, which came right after science, I sat behind Louisa. People called her Lou for short. She had red hair, brightly inquisitive eyes, and hands that gestured energetically when she talked. She'd adopted the habit of tipping back her chair and tossing questions at me, and so

I gradually came to trust she really did want to talk to me: "Are you reading the *Merchant of Venice* for English too? I love Shakespeare. It's so dramatic." "What did you do on the weekend? My mom's friend took us to the art gallery. It was amazing!"

Louisa was impressed by the goldfish experiment Meredith and I had embarked on. She called it "ambitious."

"We don't have a clue what we're doing," I assured her. "It's ridiculous."

One morning, gravely, but hurriedly, so as to get the details out before the fierce Mademoiselle Vachon began conducting class, I told her what had happened to Meredith's fish.

She laughed. "What a story!"

I was startled. Then I laughed too. Sure, it was tragic for the fish, but the creatures weren't exactly known for their longevity. Hadn't we all flushed one or two down the toilet, or seen a sitcom goldfish funeral, its tongue-in-cheek solemnity? I stopped noticing Meredith, stopped looking for her telltale slouch when I slipped into science class or walked, heart clenched, into the cafeteria that teemed with students I didn't know. It seems cruel, in retrospect. You might even say foolhardy. The things I might have learned, the fastidious scientist I might have become, pushing onward with that studious girl. But I didn't want Meredith anymore. I'd found a better prospect, off I went.

Part One

ONE

Seize the Day

ON MY JACKET THAT NIGHT I WORE A BUTTON WITH A single word on it: *Believe*. It was a gift from Lou. I'd pinned it on the wool coat I wore in winter, on my backpack in summer, and now on the jacket I wore in fall.

The pin was meant to be about Christmas. You know, don't give up on it just because the whole Santa thing is a scam, and possibly the virgin birth, too. Its significance transcended the holiday because that word, for us, had become an overriding philosophy. *Believe*. In life, the world, yourself, the people you love. We made a habit of believing in things: it felt rebellious to resist the cynicism all around us. We put truck in fate. In unseen forces. In myth and its latent powers. Yet I find no model for the great friendship of my youth in the old stories and legends. We weren't heroes or warriors. There was, in our tale, no passionate display of battlefield grief. No sacrifice of honour, family, money, freedom, or opportunity. No courageous offer to exchange one life for another, a profession of devotion so pure it might procure the mercy of a god.

At eighteen, in our final year of high school—in those days, high school in Ontario took five long years—Louisa and I were taking on the school board. It wasn't as if we'd planned it. In our system, if you were able to maintain a course mark of B or higher, your teacher could exempt you from writing the final exam. As far as we knew, it had always been thus. You didn't need to be a genius to have gotten this far in high school without ever having faced a final. I had never written one, and neither had Lou.

But not long into the fall term, *kabam*. We were told the exemption policy had been abolished over the summer. All students would write finals, no matter what. What followed was like what happens when some bozo at city hall decides to ban road hockey. Or when someone wants to tear down a historic fire hall—with its bright red garage and impressive hose tower—and replace it with a strip mall.

"Damn them."

"I can't *imagine* being here in June."

"Do you have any idea how profoundly that will suck?"

"I start my summer job in June. I'm committed. And I need the money for school!"

"It's pointless. Fucking pointless."

"They could have warned us."

Rants like this went on over trays of fries and lunch-hour games of euchre. One day someone said, "Are they allowed to do this without warning us?" Someone else said, "Can we do something about it?" One of those gazes passed between Lou and me. Later that day, when a classmate stopped us in the hall and said she had an idea, we barely let her finish her sentence before leaning in with ideas of our own.

Before we knew it, we'd helped launch a movement, an anti-final-exam brigade known as S.A.F.E.: Students

Against Final Exams. Our arsenal included a tight crew of fellow student allies and a few secret weapons (sympathetic teachers who coached us on the sly). We delivered roaring speeches—well, Lou did—littered the school newspaper with passionate opinion pieces, sent a petition around the cafeteria lunch period after lunch period. Finally, the school board agreed to consider our case. It was all very official. A presentation from S.A.F.E. was slotted into the agenda for the October board meeting. That meant us: Lou and me.

On the evening in question, I drove my mom's emerald-green Pacer in rain-soaked gloom toward Lou's. The Pacer was a small bulbous car our other friends called the Fishbowl. Sean, my older brother, revealing an initiative that I suspected wasn't quite the sort my parents hoped for, had installed extra speakers, and a tiny racing-style steering wheel in place of the regular one. Driving the car made me feel slightly ridiculous in a way that I liked, but on this occasion, I was tense. I passed through the leafy suburbs along our polluted Great Lake, catching the occasional putrid whiff from the slaughterhouse in our end of town.

The second I pulled into Lou's driveway, she rushed out the door and plopped into the passenger seat, clicked her seatbelt and nodded.

"Wow," I said. "Hi."

I was truly impressed. Usually when I was picking Lou up, I had to ring the bell and stand shifting from foot to foot in the hallway while she darted about looking for socks, lipstick, a scarf, all while bemoaning her latest dismal test results in finite math to her mom, who'd have just come in from work, or, if her mom *wasn't* home yet, shouting at her brothers to remember to do their homework. And maybe the dishes. (That was wishful thinking.)

She was all business tonight, however. Her mouth was set in a grimly determined line—just how mine felt.

"Ready?"

"Ready."

I swung the Fishbowl out of the drive and guided it through the wet streets toward the squat brick building where we were to face the school trustees.

I didn't want to jinx us with a careless move; I drove carefully, hands at ten and two. I kept glancing at my hands to make sure they weren't shaking. No music. Neither of us spoke. We were armed with a three-page brief containing four appendices. Classes had ended hours before, but we still wore our neatly pinned kilts topped with white blouses and navy cardigans: the uniform at our Catholic high school. Had I known the Berlin Wall was a few weeks from crumbling, I might have felt encouraged: power to the people!

Or I might have thought, *Look at us, a couple of spoiled brats half a world away, fighting our guts out against a few measly tests. Seriously?*

But no. My sense of injustice was way too heightened to allow for such perspective.

I parked. The clock on the dash said 7:28 p.m. Two minutes to spare. Before Lou had come into my life, four years earlier, I'd never been late or even nearly late for anything. The floor of the bedroom I shared with my sister, Wendy, had yet to disappear beneath heaps of clothing and binders and magazines. I'd been orderly, reliable. Cautious. A child.

The rain was now teeming. "Ready to run?"

"Bad idea," said Lou. "More raindrops hit you that way. It's like you're"—she thrust her arms forward, nearly whacking the windshield—"rushing right into them."

"That's ridiculous. If you run, you're in it for less time."

Louisa gripped the handle on the passenger door. "Let's find out."

When people talk about "dumb faith," they don't mean it's stupid to have faith. They mean that faith, when it truly exists, equals clarity. A wordless knowing that I still remember and reach for, though I understand now that I really knew—and still know—next to nothing. I believe accepting that strange state of unknowing is what it means to grow up. I mean, I think I believe this. If I can claim to have grown up at all, I haven't come this way peacefully. I just wanted to stay in that land of possibility that Lou and I had made, a place where—maybe, if you stayed calm and focused—you could dodge raindrops. Or outrun them. (Or somehow a little of both.) I'm tempted to say that even now, some days are all about trying to go back there, or fighting the urge to return—but I'm not sure that's true. I look at the teens and almost-teens in my sphere; I look at my own son, much younger, brimming; at my husband, siblings, parents, nieces, nephews; and, as intently as at all of these, at the friends I have now, and I wonder: What is possible, within these lives of ours? What might we make of them? Are any of us realistic about this? Maybe not, and maybe that is for the best.

I grabbed our documents, tucked them in my jacket, and bolted. Under the small overhang at the entrance I turned, dripping, to see Lou strolling through the parking lot. She was drenched. She held up her arms and laughed.

"You're a freak."

"It was just a theory."

She took cover beside me, her glistening nose inches from mine. I shielded my mouth with my hands. I spoke through my fingers. "Are we really doing this?"

She took my elbow and steered me around. A raindrop swung from her nose. "We're doing this."

INSIDE, A HUNDRED OR SO FELLOW STUDENTS, ALSO IN uniform, sat, stood, or slouched against the wall. Some were with adults, presumably their parents. It was strange to see them attached to unrecognizable grown-ups. We hadn't dared hope for so many: they barely fit in the room. Louisa nudged me. I nudged back.

My mother and father sat on padded chairs in the front row, trying not to appear worried. In his breast pocket Dad had tucked a mini tape recorder that would later accompany me to Ryerson Polytechnic Institute and support me through reporting assignments for years. Tonight, on a tiny cassette, it would capture, through the woollen weave of his jacket, the muffled sounds of our protest. "In case you ever wanted a record of what you did," he would later tell me, handing me the lozenge-sized tape, labelled in his right-slanting script: *Anita and Louisa, School Board Fight, October, 1989.* I still have it, and listening to it, I see Lou: bent over, jotting some notes, poised, fearless, and entirely self-contained. On her, the kilt-blouse combo hangs smooth and sharp, even after its trip through the rain; it nearly achieves business-suit status. On me, a damp wool skirt and a wonkily tucked-in shirt.

The carpeted room had that hushed, deadened quality I've since come to associate with all chambers of local politics. The dustless board table was a large horseshoe with trustees seated along three sides. Lou and I made our way to one end and sat beside the student from the other Catholic high school in the region. The chairman was seated directly across, rifling through papers. Before each board member sat a shiny nameplate, beside which a microphone snaked up through a hole in the brown tabletop. The nameplates and microphones, even the pitcher of water and stack of plastic cups, set there by an unseen hand prior to our arrival, unnerved me. They seemed to represent an entire system of operations beyond my comprehension: the invisible bureaucracy, the machinery of society grinding away below perception.

We'd carefully planned our dual presentation, Lou delivering one half of the brief and me the other. I tried to catch her eye; I needed reinforcement, a nod of encouragement, at least a little whispered joke about the trustee with the big hair who was shooting us the evil eye, as though we were drug dealers in the making. I sat and willed her to look up. Nothing. Lou was busy getting into character. I was on my own.

Her arm flickered and there was a sheet of paper on my lap, as though it'd blown there. It read *Carpe Diem!* in that excited Louisa scrawl, engulfing the page. When I looked up, she was grinning a grin that said we would win.

THIS WAS OUR FINAL STRETCH OF HIGH SCHOOL. FOR YEARS, we'd had a routine. We'd head to her house or mine after school and rummage in the cupboards, desperate, like stray cats. At her place, we'd make steaming bowls of Mr. Noodles with cheese sprinkled on top. We'd sit at the kitchen table twirling the dripping noodles and listening to Billy Joel, R.E.M., INXS, Tracy Chapman, U2. At my house, we'd eat slices of baloney and cheese on English muffins, heated to sizzling in the microwave. We'd engage with or avoid our respective siblings, depending. If we weren't overloaded with homework, Louisa would beg to watch *Anne of Green Gables*, which Dad had recorded off the CBC.

"No way. Not again."

"We'll fast-forward. We'll just watch that scene."

"It won't be worth it without the buildup."

"Okay!"

"Lou—no—"

"From the beginning."

"Oh my God."

"You'll thank me. This will enrich your life."

She'd spring from the couch and slide the tape into our clunky VCR. Classical music would waft into the room. There was Megan Follows on the screen in period clothing, wandering through the woods passionately reciting "The Lady of Shalott," and I knew I wasn't going anywhere until the church picnic, when Gilbert suavely arrives on the scene.

Lou didn't care that the TV series was different from the novels, or about the way books two and three had been collapsed unceremoniously into a ninety-minute script. She'd only read the first book after I nagged her, and had yet to venture beyond it, into the heady upsets of, say, *Anne of Windy Poplars*. For Lou, the attraction wasn't even about Anne, supposedly her kindred redhead. All Lou really cared about was Jonathan Crombie, the saucy-eyed actor who played Gilbert Blythe. She couldn't get enough of Crombie's interpretation of the wink Gilbert bestows upon Anne, the new girl who's caught his eye, at the end of the potato sack race. "Here it comes."

"There. Look!"

"Louisa, you're obsessed."

He tumbles at the end of the race, his dark hair flopping. He laughs and catches Anne's eye. There. Down it goes. *Wink.* Anne lifts her chin and marches off, disgusted.

"He's so hot. I have to see that again."

She'd aim the remote, and everything would wobble backward. Then, again, the moment on the grass, that oh-so-casual dare to look back. By the fourth or fifth replay, I'd feel it as keenly as she did. The flutter of Crombie's eyelid grazing the back of my neck, the backs of my calves, causing my insides to lightly flip, and flip again.

Now, though, mere months from graduation, we were far too occupied for the likes of Gilbert Blythe. We'd returned to classes after the summer with a kind of internal fever, a creeping weariness of the morning bus, the hallway scene. Our pending escape from high school felt achingly just beyond reach. We took stuff on. Louisa was editing the yearbook, I the school newspaper. Plus, Lou did drama, and ran for student council. (I was chief helper for her campaign.) Lou, drawn toward a broadcasting career, had started volunteering at Burlington Cablenet. She began hosting a show on local culture: they'd send her out with a sound team to fairs and festivals. I aimed for life as a writer and figured the only way I might reliably make a living was in journalism. I wrote some stories for the youth page of the *Burlington Post*. The page editor was encouraging and helped me set up an interview with one of my favourite MuchMusic vjs. We met at a breakfast joint on Queen Street, in downtown Toronto. I have no recollection of what we talked about, but the sense of possibility I drew from the experience was profound. I'd grasped the power of the question—the vast difference between posing one and letting it slide, or forever hauling it around.

On a September afternoon, we'd walked into a musty school portable and encountered Mr. Lawlor, the school's law teacher (for real). He had an unruly moustache and thick glasses that seemed to want to jump right off his nose. Off the top of his head, he quoted, "I went to the woods because I wanted to live deliberately. I wanted to live deep and suck out all the marrow of life. To put to rout all that was not life. And not, when I came to die, discover that I had not lived." *Suck the marrow!* The line tore into me; it was alive, the jaws and throat of the very idea it contained. From two aisles away, I looked intently at Lou and she looked back. We shared one of those burning stares that would pass between us when a discovery had been made. Lou put up her hand. "Excuse me, Mr. Lawlor. What was the name of that book?"

His moustache twitched. He noticed her pen poised over her notebook. Then his eyes flashed across the room and he noticed mine. He'd caught the invisible line between us. "*Walden*." He said it slowly, enunciating, pausing while he wrote on the board. "Henry David Thoreau. Take it out of the library. Thoreau became a champion of civil disobedience. Do any of you have any idea what that means? Civil disobedience means to follow one's principles, even if they go against the laws of the land."

So, this was a law lesson after all. Mr. Lawlor ran his classes like a late-night talk show. He replicated David Letterman's "mailbag" segment, encouraging students to send postcards, addressed to his dingy portable classroom, when they went out of town. He seldom lectured; he'd sneak a lesson up on you when you thought you were talking about—or ferociously debating—something that had nothing to do with school. He handed out a news article about a nineteen-year-old university student who'd had a great deal to drink, and then fallen down a flight of stairs and drowned in his own puke. Obviously, the story hit home. The incident had sparked calls for a new law that would place responsibility for "overdoing it" in the hands of the seller of the booze, or even the host of a party. Would such a law be just? Practical? Whose job was it to cut you off? Your friends? The bartender? Yourself? I was appalled by the idea that it should be someone else's legal duty to protect me from my own stupidity—and said as much. Which of course led to questions about other laws and bylaws created in a similar spirit. There were interruptions. There was finger-pointing, near-shouting. Class flew by. Day after day, it flew. There was Meech Lake to contend with. The Charter of Rights and Freedoms and its sticky notwithstanding clause. I'd had some good teachers, as well as my share of duds, but Mr. Lawlor was the first who managed to break down the school's metaphorical brick wall: to make what we were doing at our desks about something more than the mark at the end of the course. We weren't just a bunch of kids in a portable. We were solving the future.

Lou and I did take *Walden* out of the library. We passed it back and forth—it was wordy and logically circular, slow-going. But we kept at it; we tried. Meanwhile, we encountered that hypnotizing Thoreau quote somewhere else: the film *Dead Poets Society*, in which professor Keating, a.k.a. Robin Williams, urges his students to "suck the marrow," to seize the day. Neil Perry, the boy with the bully father, was ach-ingly beautiful. We watched the film again and again. We wrote key phrases in the writing journals we kept for our Writer's Craft English class, taught by Mr. Lucey, another kindred spirit, as we'd come to identify (in honour of Anne Shirley) anyone who "got it." We took the lines in like a challenge, a creed. *Carpe diem.* Seize the day.

We didn't expect the chance to put all this to the test. It had fallen into our laps, as if summoned.

THE BOARD ROOM WAS SILENT AS WE MADE OUR CASE. WE questioned the value of this extra exam experience. We quoted a famous education report's recommendation that "such arbitrary measures of achievement and the concepts of promotion and failure should be removed from the schools." Once, en route between classes, a history teacher had ushered us into an empty classroom and whispered urgently, "Hall-Dennis. Look it up. You didn't hear it from me." Even now, I feel the intoxication of revolution—or what passed for revolution in our mostly comfortable existence. There was actual documented research on the dubious merits of exams as teaching tools. The system wasn't necessarily designed with our best interests in mind. Anything—*any-thing*—could be questioned.

Finally, after what seemed like hours, the chair put the matter to a vote. We watched as the hands shot up. Of the fourteen members of the board, eleven voted in our favour—that is, to defer the matter till the following year and reinstate the old policy in the interim. We had saved ourselves from the scourge of finals! But our crusade had become about more than exams: it had become about having a say in the decisions that would affect our lives.

A few weeks later, shockingly and improbably, the Berlin Wall fell. Between these two triumphs of democracy—our tiny one and that huge one—we were galvanized. We found ourselves following the news, reading the papers. I started watching the *The Journal* on the CBC every night with my dad, and considered Barbara Frum, who did not so much interview her subjects as firmly pin them down, a fearless seeker of truth. Lou and her pals in drama class wrote a play, built around tableaus and a chorus, called *Der Mauer*, about a mother whose son had been killed trying to escape East Berlin. Lou had a monologue as the mother, and I would listen to her practice in the evenings: "A boy went over the wall last night. The boy ran toward the wall with such determination…The shot echoed through the misty night air. Strangers mourned and friends cried out in anguish…Let me ask you this: Do you remember what freedom is?"

I wondered about our relatives in Poland. My grand-parents had left in 1938, before the war, and contact with family there was patchy. "Will things change for them?" I asked Mom one night.

"I don't think so," she said. "Not for a good long while."

In history class we were asked to make a list of historical figures we'd invite to a dinner party. I wrote: "I will have a dinner party with Henry David Thoreau, Joan of Arc, and a student activist killed in the 1989 uprising in China. They will discuss their own frustrations with government and their radical actions and ideas that challenged society."

"Someday someone will put you on a list like this," I said to Lou.

"As what? A star from Burlington Little Theatre?"

"No way. Prime minister of Canada."

It was an off-the-cuff remark, but very quickly—I felt it happen to both of us—we started to think: Well, why not? Why the fuck not?

"You'd sure beat Mulroney."

"The chin, for one thing."

"Exactly. And free trade."

"He's so arrogant."

"He's in love with George Bush. It's embarrassing."

"We need a leader who can think for himself."

"Who isn't playing golf all the time."

During the exam battle we'd gotten permission from the principal to hold a massive class meeting in the cafeteria. We split the duties. Lou spoke, and I read the letter we— mostly I—had composed and sent to the trustees. The letter was good; I knew that. But it was Lou who sent a current through the room. She was comfortable on that stage that was usually reserved for talent shows. She was capable of delivering a rousing call to our friends—and to those who didn't care to be our friends: "We've been had. We have to do something. We CAN do something!" I could see it, I really could. Louisa on Parliament Hill, her red hair blazing in the sunlight before the Peace Tower, rallying the country to some great cause.

For now, though, we were high school students in a southern Ontario suburb. We had homework, tests—and lives outside of school, where things kept moving along their own paths despite our grand ambitions. Lou, her mom, and her brothers left their house near us for a place halfway across town. I hated that she wasn't close by anymore. But she was back in her old neighbourhood, where she'd lived before we met, down the road from our high school. I got into the habit of walking home with her after class. If we had no urgent homework, we'd head downstairs to watch Oprah, her little Shih Tzu, Prose, curled on the couch between us. Lou would drive me home after her mom got home from work. Or I'd stay for supper and on into the evening: we'd spread our schoolwork over the kitchen table and sit there working with plates of cookies and cups of tea.

One night we were pouring over some photos. I'd found them in the old cabinet in our living room and stuffed them in my backpack to show Lou.

"Look at my mom," I was saying. "She was nineteen when Sean was born."

In the photo, Mom is lying on the bed in the farmhouse where she grew up. Sean (later of the rogue steering-wheel installation) is on her belly, head-up, caterpillar style, staring at the camera. He has a chunk of her blue shirt gripped in one of his fists. She grins, watching him, her dark brown hair spilling over the pillow. I imagined, looking at it, that she was surprised by the strength of his grip. She was thinking: I made this creature? He came from me? She was just a girl herself. She could have been the babysitter, the older sister, a cousin.

Lou would turn nineteen in August. In winter, I'd hit that age too. Her wide eyes mirrored mine. "Your mom never had a chance."

We were cutting into a block of orange cheddar Lou's mother had brought home with the groceries.

"There's no way I'm doing that."

"Not before twenty-five."

"At least."

We started in on the math: When would we finish university? How many years would we need beyond that before having a family wouldn't sabotage everything?

There was a clanking, or a splash, or an exasperated sigh. Some noise drew our eyes to the sink. Lou's mother whirled around, like she'd appeared from nowhere. Her hair was a slightly lighter red than Lou's: it framed her smooth brow in a wash of waves and curls. Her eyes, usually delicate and kind, were like arrowheads, her faint eyebrows pulled back like bowstrings.

I liked Lou's mom. We could pretty much ask or tell her anything and get what felt like an honest response, not something edited for underage consumption. And she would ask us pointed questions: "Did you kiss him?" "How was it?" When, years back, I'd finally given up on Paul Harvey, who hadn't spoken to me more than twice during ten months of me walking past his desk in grade nine, she'd waved a hand in the air and said, "Don't sweat it, Anita. There'll always be another bus."

She'd had her share of struggles. Her father had died of Hodgkin's lymphoma when she was just seven years old. Now she was navigating the tricky terrain of the split family, raising three kids with an ex-husband who lived across town. (Lou and her brothers often stayed with their dad on weekends.) After the divorce, she'd gone back to school to become a computer technician—she was smart; she knew where the best jobs would be. But money was still tight. Now she stared at us hard. We stared back. The half-eaten block of cheese sat before us on the table. I remembered the time Louisa's brothers had eaten all the cheese within a day of her grocery shopping, and—we were all in the car, she was driving us somewhere—she'd slammed the steering wheel and said, "That's it. I quit!"

I braced myself.

"You can't plan your life, girls." She flung each word. "You think you can. But you have no idea."

Then she left the room.

"God, what's her problem?"

"Who knows."

We shrugged. Parents. Of course we could plan. That was clearly where *they'd* all gone wrong.

TWO

One-Celled Creatures

IT'S WEIRD HOW ABRUPTLY LIFE CAN CHANGE. DO I MEAN abruptly, or imperceptibly? I didn't realize, at first, that anything of note was going on in grade-nine French, on our third day of school.

That was the day I first spoke to Louisa. I should say, she spoke to me.

The timetable still baffled me. I'd slipped into class flush-faced and nearly late. I sat in the only empty seat, behind a redheaded girl against the far wall. The wall was a pale yellow, and next to it, the girl's hair looked like an explosion in a comic strip.

The redhead had brushed past me that morning in the crowded hallway. I didn't yet know her name, but I'd noticed her. Like most of the others around us, her kilt was cut to the perfect length, the hem kissing the upper ridge of her knee. Mine dragged along my calves, weighing me down like a wet towel. I could have killed Sean, who was in grade ten, for not warning me that a long kilt was not cool. How would I convince Mom to shorten it now, without her accusing me of "following the crowd"? Of course I was. And so what? Mom didn't get that in some contexts, fitting in was just a harmless way to make life easier. Way easier.

I faced forward and opened my three-ring binder. "Oh no!" I'd completely forgotten about the course outline we were instructed to bring to class, signed by our parents. The page sat there in the rings, untouched since I'd placed it there two mornings before.

Mademoiselle Vachon, a tall, sturdy blonde with a musical voice and menacing expression, was gliding down the aisles. She seemed to have risen straight out of the rabbit hole in *Alice in Wonderland*.

"Believe me, my little retarded amoebas, there will be consequences if you fail this simple instruction." She'd said these exact words two days earlier, in English, though this was French class. "Retarded amoebas" would be her pet name for us, she had carefully explained, because she'd long ago learned to expect little from her grade nines. (Though not quite so shocking in 1985 as it would be now, it was still a startling thing for a teacher to say.) Grade nines were clueless, she said. She hoped we would rise above this reality. As a class, we had discussed the meaning of the word *amoeba*. The redhead had been the only one who knew, or admitted to knowing, that an amoeba was a one-celled creature.

Mademoiselle Prose. That's what the teacher had called her. *Merci, Mademoiselle Prose*, she'd said crisply.

I blinked at the sheet uselessly, hoping the signature would appear. "Shit!"

The redhead spun around. "Forge it," she said. Her eyes were blue, but not the usual sky blue: deep and rich, like new jeans right out of the wash.

"Huh?"

"Your mother's signature. Forge it."

Mademoiselle was getting nearer, moving up our aisle like an officer conducting inspection. I pictured a filing cabinet in a musty basement somewhere labelled *Retarded Amoebas*, in which she stored all her grade nine French students' documents. If I succeeded, my forgery would remain in one of the cabinet's dark drawers, silently condemning me until the end of time.

A shadow fell on my desk. I lifted my head, looked straight into those unforgiving eyes and said, "*Pardon, Mademoiselle, mais, j'ai oublié.*"

All her features fell into a thin, stern line. She leaned toward me.

"*Remets-le à moi lundi.*" She enunciated each word.

With that she was gone. I caught my breath. I watched the redhead display her own signed sheet, preparing to tell her that I didn't have it in me. I was a wimp. It wasn't my fault. When the teacher was gone, she turned and flashed me a smile.

"Way to go," she whispered. "Great thinking!"

"It was an accident."

"Well it worked! She was impressed by your French."

"I'm such an idiot."

"No. You're obviously very smart."

This was new. Someone who *liked* that you were smart.

She told me her name was Louisa. "Louis*a*, not Louise."

I couldn't help thinking of *Anne of Green Gables*, and the *e* on her name and how much it mattered. The *a* at the end of *Louisa* changed everything. It gave her name a jauntiness, a lift.

Louisa's mother's name was Louise. Her grandmother's name was Mary Lou. Louisa hated it when people got their names mixed up, but she liked the pattern. She wondered what she could name her own daughter, though, that would match her mother and grandmother's names.

"Your daughter?" We were whispering, me leaning slightly forward toward the back of her head, Louisa tilting her face just barely toward the wall. Anyone watching would have thought we were listening intently to Mademoiselle.

"When I have one."

"Oh." I frowned. "Not Lola. I have a second or third cousin with that name. I was the junior bridesmaid at her wedding—and I barely even know her."

"Junior bridesmaid?"

I shrugged. "I think it's a Polish thing."

"I was thinking maybe Lucy."

"That could work. Or Lucia. There's a Lucia in my history class."

"Lucia." Her forehead wrinkled, and she touched her pen to her bottom lip, considering.

LOUISA STARTED SLIPPING ME NOTES DURING LECTURES, and when we passed each other in the hallways. She taught me to fold them into neat little packets, like I imagined girls from the turn of the century might have done.

At home, I'd tuck them into the top drawer of the small pine desk where I did my homework, most of which I found tedious. But I enjoyed conjugating verbs into the new tense we were learning in French: *imparfait*. I fell into the verbs' rhythmic patterns.

J'étais. Tu étais. Il/elle était. Nous étions. Vous étiez. Ils étaient.

Were. We were. Mademoiselle said English speakers—and retarded amoebas—had a tough time with this: the difference between *passé composé* and *imparfait*. A past action started and finished in a given timeframe, one-time-only, as opposed to something habitual, continuous, ongoing. *En anglais, cette idée n'existe pas.* But I got it. I thought I got it. *Imparfait* was how things had been "once upon a time." In the days before something had changed. In my case, in grade eight, for example. Before high school.

J'étais toujours seule. J'étais toujours dans un livre.

Would you say that in French? *I was always in a book?* I leaned back in my chair, wobbling on its hind legs. My eyes wandered by Mary and Jesus in their plastic frame, a poster of Daryl Sittler leaning on his stick, the red blinds. I eased the chair back down to all fours, got up, and slid my copy of *Anne of Green Gables* off the bookshelf. Standing, I started flipping through, skimming. I stopped when I found the scene when Anne and Diana meet for the first time and walk through the Barrys' garden, amid peonies and daffodils. Diana was quiet, like me. Reserved, like me. A brunette, like me.

I sat down on the bed railing and began to read.

SINCE I WAS YOUNG, MY MOTHER HAD BEEN ENSCONCED in a lively trio: herself, Barbara Hartnett, and Anne Durham. They taught Sunday school at church, took turns hosting Christmas parties for our three families, and were forever re-enacting a scene in which they tried to give each other money. That, I understood, was the main symbol of friendship between adults: wanting to pay. As familiar to me as grocery store errands was the drive to Mrs. Hartnett's, about five minutes away in a treed neighbourhood on winding streets like ours, yet entirely foreign. This would often occur the morning after a get-together between our families, or after our parents had gone out for a steak supper with the Hartnetts, leaving us home with a babysitter. I imagined Mr. Hartnett, as the meal came to an end, slipping the bill into his lap while Dad was refilling the ladies' wine glasses, and then quickly catching the waiter's eye. Mom and Dad would protest, but Barbara would shush them. "Just accept it for once." The next day, after I'd finished my bowl of cereal, Mom, her lips pursed, would hustle me into the car, and we'd head to the Hartnetts' house, white with black trim and a garage. Mom would slow up by the curb, dig in her purse, pull out an envelope, and say sternly, "Don't ring the bell." She'd keep the car running while I ran up and tucked the envelope into the mailbox with an end sticking out, so someone would know it was there. I avoided looking at the door or windows—neither see nor be seen—whirled around, hurried back down the walkway, jumped into the car, and pulled the door shut. Before I'd reached for my seatbelt, Mom would be veering into a three-point-turn.

These secret cash drop-offs were the most dramatic elements of her social life, as far as I could see. Otherwise there was a great deal of sitting around and talking. Mom and her friends sat on kitchen chairs, living room couches, lawn chairs—and it was as if someone hit Play on the conversation even before their bums hit the seats. They did not finish one conversation and start up a new one. They had a single conversation that never ceased, that they put on Pause when someone rose to go home and picked up seamlessly a week or two or a month later. It looked like nothing much was going on, just three women at a table. But in the midst of planning the week's Sunday school lesson they might suddenly be helpless with laughter over the time Mom and Dad got the car stuck in the wheat field at the farm and had to get Uncle Ed to help dig them out.

"We told *Tata* that Sandy was giving me driving lessons."

"I'll bet he was."

"What *were* you doing?" I asked. I'd wandered into the kitchen for a glass of orange juice. Three faces locked on mine. Mom snorted. Whenever she couldn't stop laughing, it went into her nose.

"Phyllis, control yourself." That was Anne. But she had covered her mouth, and her whole body shook.

Mom held a hand to her chest and breathed deeply. "Aren't you supposed to be doing your homework?"

The atmosphere changed when Mrs. Hartnett and Mrs. Durham were around. Mom became more lighthearted, the air around her at the same time more charged. I envied Mom these friends and their bursts of laughter, their sudden judgments, the plots they worked and reworked while nursing cups of Maxwell House. Obviously, especially as you got older, you needed people around you who knew about that time you got caught in the wheat field with your boyfriend—people who dared to love and mock you at the same time, who would call you on your shit and who, by a knowing glance or a well-timed remark, could turn your disasters into jokes.

Dad, too, had friends who were woven tightly into our lives. When he moved from Nova Scotia to Ontario in his early twenties, he boarded with a family in Hamilton. He became close with the two sons, and by the time we kids came along we were ensconced into the family as though we were actual relations. We called the older couple Ma and Pa and thought of them as our "extra" grandparents. When we were with them, Dad wasn't Sandy, he was Sam. They'd given him this nickname to avoid confusion with one of the brothers' wives, also a Sandy. It was jarring to hear someone call "Sam" and see Dad turn around. It was as if, through the prism of these friendships, he was a separate person from the one we knew.

APPARENTLY, HOWEVER, MOM AND DAD DIDN'T WANT *ME* to have a friend. At least, not a chatty redhead who had divorced parents and didn't go to church. Or maybe didn't go.

"Well do they?"

"How should I know?"

"I haven't seen them there."

"They just moved here, I told you that. They used to live near St. Raph's."

That was short for Raphael. Our church was St. Pat's, short for Patrick. Sean and I had convinced our parents it was all right to show up for Mass there in jeans. The important thing, we argued, was that we were there—and wasn't it what was on the inside, not the outside, that really mattered? Was God really worried about our clothes? St. Pat's was a low-slung, brown brick building with wall-to-wall carpeting, and hymn lyrics projected onto the wall during Mass. As in every Catholic church, a crucifix hung behind the altar—except ours wasn't exactly a crucifix. Our Jesus, carved from a pale, sunny wood, was not nailed to his cross but rising off it, his muscular arms opened triumphantly, as though ready to give us all a massive, post–Vatican II hug.

"Hmm," said Mom. That meant she was thinking about the reason they'd moved: Louisa's parents' recent divorce.

"We just met," I said. "It's not like I know her life story."

"Watch your tone, young lady."

"Sorry." But I hadn't changed my tone. I was just anxious to get over to Louisa's. That's why I had to endure all these questions.

"Next time, she comes here."

Fun, I thought, *she'll love it, the house where no one is allowed to do anything*. But I had won. "Okay, sure," I said.

"Be home at four."

"It's almost two now!"

"Would you rather not go at all?"

I marched down the driveway. You'd think I was asking her to let me hitchhike to Montreal. I started down the sidewalk and followed the curve of our road down toward the lake. It was a sunny Saturday in early September, the remains of summer lingering. The warm, slanting daylight deepened the reds and browns of the brick-walled homes.

I loosely timed the walk, so I'd know when to leave to get home on time. It took about fifteen minutes, crossing in front of Skyway Arena, winding down the laneway at the back of Skyway Plaza and through the smell of the dumpster behind the A&P. Beyond the plaza and through the vacant lot at the corner, the houses across the street gave way to a park along the water. Distant oil tankers stealthily glided through Lake Ontario, on their way to the Petro-Canada yards nearby.

I'd been to this park many times. I'd taught my younger brother, Matthew, to skip stones here, coaching him to keep the stone flat-as-could-be between his thumb and forefinger. But more often than not, I came to the park alone. I'd scramble down the tiny cliff to the beach covered in smooth stones, broken bottles, and fish skeletons, and stand with my hands in my pockets, my eyes on the water, imagining the opposite shore that was too far too see, and my mind on the unknown events that would collect and glom into what I would, eventually, call my life. Over these moments drifted a nagging question of why I didn't feel in it yet, my life.

I came to a little sign with a carving of a sailboat. *Village by the Lake*. I looked carefully down the corresponding row of townhouses. She hadn't given me an address. "I can't remember it yet," she'd said. "It's the one with the bay window."

Right, I thought, they'd only just moved. I didn't yet know this was a prime example of Lou's essential nature: gloss over practicalities (exact address), focus on what brings joy (beautiful window). I had to ask what a bay window was.

"It's the kind you can sit in," she said excitedly.

There was one house with a large, black-framed window jutting out proudly from a wall of coppery yellow brick. I approached and stood before the door. Two hours suddenly seemed like forever. I hated my jeans: they didn't fit properly and were the cheap kind that never faded.

Louisa's mother would be out. Her brothers were staying with their dad for the weekend. We'd have the place to ourselves. This was the part I had not told Mom.

I lifted the knocker, snapping it down into a satisfactory clang. I shuffled back and forth, listening for movement on the other side.

"WE'RE NOT ALLOWED TO BE IN HERE."

Her voice was low, conspiratorial. "Come on. I want to show you something." She strode into the living room and flopped on the spotless white sofa. Barefoot, she wore a baggy T-shirt and jeans, frayed along the cuffs. A pale foot rose from the floor, slipped beneath her faded pant leg and disappeared.

I stood on the threshold of the pristine room. The couch was as white as a porcelain sink. Louisa waved me in with her hand, her head, her hair, her movements a blur of reds against the cushions.

I crossed the room. On the couch, I wondered if my pants were dirty. I sat very still.

Louisa leaned over the glass-topped coffee table and turned the cover on a thick book with a satiny white cover. A starry-eyed man and woman smiled out from the first page, the woman in a long white gown and the man in a tuxedo. It was a wedding album. I had a kajillion older cousins, most of them married. The weddings I'd attended had begun to blend into one big event in my mind, where I listened to goofy speeches and then worked up the nerve to dance. I wondered how, or if, I could say "no thanks" to this little wedding tour.

"They were so beautiful," Louisa said dreamily.

They looked like any wedding couple to me: a little false, like dolls. Knowing how things turned out probably didn't help. But as Lou turned the pages, I found myself admiring this youthful, smiling bride and groom—her slim giant of a dad and her glamorous, redheaded mother. Sitting next to me, thigh to thigh, her blue jeans melding into mine, Louisa had cast a spell. She found the part inside of me designed to believe in things: good things, happy things. Found it and flipped the dial to ON.

I wondered what her mother would do if she arrived home. I imagined her standing in the hallway glaring at this strange girl sitting on her new couch, leafing through her wedding album, dredging up her past. "Did you scam this from your mom?"

"She doesn't mind."

"We make fun of pictures of my parents," I said. It was true. It was all: *Get a load of those burns, Dad! Check out that hair on Mom—what did you do, bleach it?* (She had. It was the sixties.)

"I didn't speak to my dad for ages after the divorce."

"Oh."

I told her about my dad's heart attack then, how he had collapsed and, when he came to, didn't recognize my mother. We sat for a moment. I thought about the weeks Dad had spent in hospital. And how Louisa's dad wasn't coming home.

"I was so mean," she said. "But I see him all the time now."

We were surrounded by delicate unicorn figurines: her mother's collection. They made me uneasy, as though I was following her through a store filled with breakable things. I told Louisa about the time I was playing with the kids across the street and was sent home by their mother because I was pulling leaves off a plant while we sat on the patio stones. I didn't even know I was doing it. I'd been absorbed in the game we were playing.

"What a bitch," Louisa said.

"But she warned me."

"You were just a kid."

It wasn't some deep dark secret. But the memory did rear up in my mind at unexpected moments: me by the plant, playing cards, a shadow falling and the woman shouting: "I told you not to touch the plants!"

Louisa turned more pages in the album, pointing out her uncles and aunts. My entire sense of the incident had been altered. I thought of how Louisa had forgiven her dad for whatever had happened, and how I wouldn't know what to say when I got home and my mother asked me what we'd done all afternoon.

"I'm going to loan you a sweater. I have one you'll like. Come on." Lou didn't allow us to simply walk out of the living room. We tilted the cushions against the armrests, smoothed the depressions where we'd been sitting, and backed into the hallway side by side, our thin bodies bent over, the palms of our hands brushing the dents of our footprints out of the carpet.

WE SAT AT THE KITCHEN TABLE IN THEIR TOWNHOUSE after school, hunched before steaming bowls of Mr. Noodles. We were still in uniform, but our beige blouses were untucked, our navy knee socks crumpled around our ankles. She was telling me about her old house, which was right around the corner from our high school.

"I loved it. It was Spanish."

"Spanish?"

"Stucco. With black shutters and railings."

They'd been there for six years, since Lou was in grade two. Before that they lived in Oakville. Coming to Burlington, she'd left a boyfriend behind.

"A boyfriend? You were what, six?"

She nodded solemnly. "Nicholas. We made up plays together. We were the mom and dad. Sometimes we had fourteen kids."

"Like the Game of Life. Those little pegs you stuck into the car—remember? You'd pile kids on top of kids—"

"No seatbelts!"

Jon, Lou's brother, came pounding down the stairs and burst into the kitchen, his hands full of dinky cars, and dumped them on the table. He started to show me how fast they could go: the bus, the taxi, the wagon, the sports car. One after the other careened off the table and clunked to the linoleum.

"Jon. Leave Anita alone. She doesn't care."

"It's okay. I don't mind." With her little brother clamouring for my attention, I felt like I actually belonged there, in

Lou's kitchen. I was part of her world. Jon grinned up at me from the floor, where he was gathering up his crashed vehicles. He began lining them up on the table. Lou kept talking. When she moved she went to St. Paul's, which always used to beat St. Pat's at volleyball. I wondered if she played. I didn't remember seeing her, but that was one of my problems in life: too chicken to look around. Or maybe just too inward. Thinking instead of noticing.

"I wasn't sporty," she said, shaking her head. "I was in theatre. It saved me." She tugged on a bunch of hair falling over her forehead. She blinked. Sighed. "It's how I made friends." She was so lonely when she first got to St. Paul's that she started giving her snack away at recess. "It was stupid. I was trying to buy friends."

"Uh, no, you were sharing."

"I thought it would make them like me." She turned to Jon. "Don't try to buy your friends, okay?" He flicked a red car with his finger. It rolled to the lip of the table and stopped.

I tried to make her see that she was being way too hard on her seven-year-old self. It's tough to credit, thirty years on, how riveting and crucial this story, and my effort to alter its meaning in her mind, felt. Louisa's loneliness in that schoolyard, her shame over the survival strategy she'd devised. But the more I tried to convince her, the less she seemed inclined to believe me.

We were already slipping into our respective roles.

THREE

Frostbite

WE WERE ON THE PHONE, ME IN THE BLUE-TILED KITCHEN with yellow-and-brown flowered wallpaper at our house, Lou in the clean, modern kitchen at theirs. I spoke with a low-lying, white-noise cloud of worry over me, one ear half-cocked toward the stairs. Any moment one of my parents might poke a head in the kitchen doorway, eye me sternly and say, loud enough for Lou to hear, "You've been on the phone long enough!"

We were caught up in a familiar rant. "She didn't show up. It was there till five o'clock!"

"What a rat."

"A rat in a kilt."

"A rat in a kilt with disgusting rat paws and a long, slimy tail."

"A rat in a kilt with disgusting rat paws and a long, slimy tail dipped in pond scum."

"Yuck."

The rat was Francesca, Lou's co-editor on the yearbook, who left all the photo cropping and layout to Lou, had yet to write a single caption, and never did a thing she'd promised.

I was beginning to think I should offer to help, but I had my own problems, mainly with the school newspaper I was meant to be editing. In truth, I wasn't much of an editor. I couldn't bring myself to spend my lunch hours recruiting reporters or interviewing the jocks about the latest volleyball game. I just wanted to eat a plate of fries or a grilled cheese sandwich, chat, and play euchre. Or sneak off to the library to read. Or, if it was a nice day, cut through the hydro right-of-way to the mall, my kilt flapping against the back of my knees and my navy socks bunching down toward my ankles with each step, the sun warming my calves.

I was about to confess all this to Louisa. When it came to all this extra-curricular mumbo-jumbo, I was as bad as Francesca the rat: some of us just weren't cut out for it. But she spoke first.

"Anyway, I found this lump." Her voice went soft and timid. "There's a lump under my arm."

I'd been slouched in a chair with my sock feet on the table. I slid them off, sat up, and said carefully into the receiver, "Are you sure? It's really a lump?"

I thought of her last health scare. There'd been several during the four years since we'd met in that long-ago French class. The incident that came to mind was several months before, toward the end of grade twelve. We'd been studying for a math test in her bedroom, sitting on the floor amid discarded clothing. Prose, the dog, was asleep on her bed, a little pillow of fur. Lou had started to cry.

"What's the matter?" She shook her head. "Louisa? What is it?" She wouldn't look up. "You can't start crying and not tell me why."

"Okay." She breathed. She was cross-legged, fiddling with her sleeve. She was wearing a thick wool sweater her grandmother had knit for her, green with a snowflake pattern around the shoulders. It was way too big. That was how we wore our sweaters, sloppy, and her grandmother was kind enough to oblige. Every year on Louisa's birthday, she'd present her with a homemade sweater large enough for a grown man, but incongruously bright or cute: one year she'd knit a little gathering of farm animals into the front panel.

The spray of freckles on Louisa's cheeks made a delicate marble pattern. Staring resolutely at her hands, she said in a throaty voice, "I think I have AIDS."

"How? You've never even had sex."

"But I had that operation."

"On the cyst? When you were twelve?"

She sniffed and wiped her nose with the back of her hand. "Yes."

"They sterilize the equipment, don't they?" I had a flash: Oh, yeah, the tainted blood scandal. But that was mainly transfusions, right? She hadn't had one of those.

"I bled a lot after the operation," she said. "They had to give me blood."

Oh. She did have a point. It was possible. But it was also possible that World War III would break out and the Soviet Union, in an effort to bomb the United States, would accidentally annihilate us instead. It was possible that my father would have another heart attack, and this time not have the chance to wake up and fail to recognize my mother. Louisa's whip-smart, beautiful mother might never find a good, solid man. Someone we knew could become paralyzed in a car accident. I might never master French and Lou might fail finite math. Neither one of us might ever get to have sex even when we wanted to, nor have enough money to go to university. One of my brothers, or one of hers, might turn bad. I might be right that one or both of my parents had a drinking problem. Another Great Depression could hit. Diet

Coke might be taken off the market. John Cusack might never make another film. No one we knew might ever come close to living up to their potential.

Lou continued, talking into her lap again. "I'm having night sweats."

"I thought AIDS just meant you got sick more easily with other things."

She shook her head firmly. "It's a symptom. I saw it on one of those stupid slides."

We'd been learning about how you could and couldn't get AIDS since elementary school, before she and I had met. Sometimes these lessons were woven into sex ed. It was complicated in Catholic school: not only was sex before marriage a big no-no, so was every kind of birth control except "natural planning." The solution was to refrain from all mention of condoms, diaphragms, IUDs, and the pill. Chapter four in our grade-ten health textbook had been glued together. I remember sitting in class with this solid block of pages between my fingers. Mrs. Dooley, a trim, athletic woman with short dark hair who wore track pants and golf shirts, stood before us, her eyes narrowed and her cheeks flared. She held the book open to the offending chapter, splayed the way the priest held the Bible during Mass.

"You all know what this chapter is about. The Appleby Roman Catholic School Board, in its wisdom, has decided I'm not allowed to bring up the information that's in here. *But*." She looked around the room, eyeing each girl in turn (phys. ed. and health was the one class we had that was not co-ed). Her eyes met mine and it was like a slap: *Wake up*. "It's my job to answer any question you ask, either during class or after. Understand? Anything."

It was a relief that a grown-up thought the rules were stupid, too.

Mrs. Dooley reiterated all the things we'd been taught before, but with more oomph. You could not get AIDS from touching someone or sitting where they'd sat or even from kissing, unless you both had seriously bleeding gums and were French kissing. We laughed. She waited for us to stop, then she said, "It requires the exchange of fluids. Not saliva. Blood. Semen. Anal sex. Oral sex. Sex without protection." She raised her eyebrows in silent translation. "Protection" equals "condom." We got it.

"If you're that worried," I said to Lou, "talk to Mrs. D. Or just get a test."

"Maybe."

I sighed. "You don't have AIDS."

"You're probably right." She seemed disappointed.

A few days later I asked her about it. She shrugged. "They're gone. The sweats."

"Really?"

She rolled her eyes. "I know, I have hypochondriac tendencies." She made it sound grand. "I try, but I can't help it." And that was that.

Now this. But you couldn't conjure a lump: either it was there or it wasn't. How big was it? Was it red, like a mosquito bite? Itchy? Sore? "Can you describe it?"

She breathed. "Well. You wouldn't see it, exactly. It's under the skin."

The timidity was gone. I tried to take in what she was saying. It was kind of loose: you could move it around. The size of a pea. Strangely, this seemed familiar, almost clichéd. Were all such lumps the size of a pea?

"Which arm?" I pressed three fingers under my left arm. The pocket there was soft and warm, a little hollow inside a circle of bones.

"It's the same arm as my scar."

"What?" I pulled my hand from my armpit. Her scar. The cyst. "The same arm?"

"Do you think that's bad?"

A shadow fell on my lap. I looked up. Mom. I'd forgotten to listen for her. I'd forgotten where I was. She was reaching for me—to take the phone away? Her hand found my left shoulder. I felt the weight of it. Her warm brown eyes found mine. *What is it?* Her mouth shaped the words. *What's the matter?* An instinct for empathy: Mom's superpower. So powerful, so giving, but sometimes misapplied, as if she were programmed to seek and soothe pain that didn't yet, or might never, exist. I had the urge to pass her the phone. *You talk to her. You figure it out.* My mind swirled around the question of Lou's scar, and the cyst that had been removed from her shoulder the year before we met. Just what *was* a cyst? Not a tumour, surely, or that's what it would have been called. So, what had its appearance meant? And why had it been so important for the doctors to cut it away?

I shrugged Mom's hand away—*later, I'll tell you later*—and clunked my elbows on the table.

It was long, so very long, before I would perceive the profound fear that—it's now so clear to me—had embedded deep within Louisa the moment her fingers alighted on that lump.

The problem was, Lou did "fear" like a lead on Broadway. She'd received a minor speeding ticket once, while zipping down one of the side streets near our high school in her mother's Nissan. She'd had no idea she was going fifty-six in a forty-kilometre-per-hour zone. Ever after, even when she wasn't at the wheel, she eyed the speedometer with the intensity of a hotly pursued bank robber—except that she wanted you to *slow down*. The point was, the ticket had unearthed one of her latent, more powerful bugaboos: how quickly control could slip from your grasp. Also on the list were guilt, ugliness, mediocre grades, and unpopularity (read: loneliness). She dreaded her mother's wrath, her father's disappointment, her two younger brothers' unhappiness and her own. She often declared that she was terrified of sex. "No, no, no." She would shake her bright red hair, her feet tucked up beneath her on the couch, the scraggly family Shih Tzu curled up in her lap. "I just can't go there. I can't." I was practiced at deflecting her scares, making light of them, especially the ones that had to do with getting sick. Louisa was so often on the verge of some perceived doom, it was hard to take her seriously.

By the time the lump turned up, more than halfway through our final year of high school, all of this was embedded into our friendship and the ways in which we conversed. "Getting" her fear would mean acknowledging it was reasonable. (Now, though, I wonder about her phantom scares: What might she have sensed, subconsciously, in her very bones?) It would mean acknowledging the way it bulged there between us, a throbbing mass of emotional experience that was rudely shoving her one way and me another, down paths that no longer easily intertwined. There was no capacity in me yet for that sort of understanding. It was my job to undermine this thing—a trifle, the size of a pea, for goodness sake.

And yet. I gripped the receiver as tightly as you grip one of those dangling straps on a city bus. Into the round black holes, to Louisa in the kitchen at the other end of town, I said, "What are you going to do?"

SOMEONE—SOME DOCTOR—DECIDED THE LUMP SHOULD be removed. The day of Louisa's surgery, our friend Esme and I were in the caf, hunched over peanut butter sandwiches. She reached across the table and touched my arm.

"I can go to the hospital with you." Esme's mom had breast cancer. It had been a year or more. She knew the ins and outs, the whole hospital rigmarole.

"Aren't you fed up with going there?"

"I don't mind."

I was grateful. She'd know where to park, what entrance to use, what to ask at the desk. I picked her up that evening in the bright green Fishbowl. Its jauntiness clashed with my mood. As we passed the Lakeshore mansions, shadows from the sturdy old maples lining the road brushed over the car. Like blessings, I thought. I hoped.

My mom often asked how things were going with Esme's mom. What treatment was she on? Was she managing okay? It was tough to say: Esme wasn't big on details. But I knew that, as the eldest, Esme had taken stuff on, cooking and housekeeping, that sort of thing. Esme's mother's name was Thérèse. She'd grown up in a French-Canadian community in northern Ontario. I missed her sing-song voice calling down when we walked in the door. "Esme! Is it you? There's iced tea in the fridge!" Now, when I went over, her mom was usually resting. We kept our voices down.

Upstairs in the hospital, Lou was wide awake and in her own room, but, her father warned us in the hallway, she was not quite herself. We stepped inside. She was sitting up in bed, wearing a baggy T-shirt and track pants. Her hair was a mess. She gasped and threw her arms open when she saw us—"You came!"—as though we hadn't seen each other in years.

"Of course! How are you?"

"You're so good to me."

"Are you sore?"

"My dad's here too. And Miles and Jon. And Mom. I'm such a lucky girl. I'm so loved. Everybody cares!"

Lou's dad, a giant teddy bear of a man, shrugged and smiled. He dug a few bills out of his wallet. "Could you girls go down and get me a coffee? And something for yourselves."

Esme steered us expertly down the hallways lined with open doorways, through the thick scent of disinfectant and the sharp, pungent, sick-room odours.

"Will she be in pain after the drugs wear off?"

"Probably," Esme said. "Anytime they cut into you, tissue gets torn."

I winced.

"But they'll give her painkillers," she added quickly. Esme had made the decision to study medicine, and possibly specialize in oncology. Her hair was pulled straight back in an elastic, and her smooth, bare forehead gleamed in the fluorescent lights as we turned into the cafeteria. There were no lines along her brow, no hints of the worries and trials that had accompanied her mom's diagnosis. I could picture her in a white lab coat, with her hair pulled back just this way and her hands linked behind her back as she peered into a microscope. Esme was capable, that's what she was. And older—older inside now than I was.

We peeled back the lids on little plastic thimbles of milk and poured the creamy liquid into our steaming paper cups of tea. "Do you think," I began, rolling an empty creamer between my thumb and forefinger, "do you think it makes a difference *where* they found the lump?"

Esme frowned. "You mean—"

"Your mom had a lump in her breast, right? Everyone knows what that can mean—but a lump in your arm? Couldn't that be—is it really…necessarily…"

She gripped a hand around my upper arm and looked straight into my eyes. "I have no idea, Anita. I don't know enough about it."

"Of course you don't. I'm sorry. You know—it's the same arm as her scar."

"Yeah. That kinda worries me too."

"Maybe a coincidence?"

"I'm sure they'll figure it out. One thing I can say is that they seem to do their best."

I nodded. Okay. They. Them. That Esme might soon be one of them was a good thing. But it meant, of course, that *they'd* all once been just like us: high school students without a clue. How had they gone from here to there, to being the people who could say whether what had just been sliced out of Lou's arm was nothing or everything? Could a few years of study really be enough? I looked at Esme's thoughtful expression as she mixed sugar into the coffee for Lou's dad and thought: For her, yes. Definitely. But not everyone was an Esme.

We pressed the plastic lids on tight and turned to catch the elevator back up to the room where Lou was easing out of her stupor.

Lying in bed that night, I thought of Louisa asleep in her hospital bed, or trying to sleep. Was she still drugged up, or wide awake and frightened? Had her mother or father stayed with her? Was there a kind nurse who popped her head in every so often, and smiled when she saw that Lou was sleeping soundly?

GRADE NINE, FOUR LONG YEARS BEFORE THE LUMP. IT was Saturday night, and Lou was sleeping over. I waited till the second period was over and Don Cherry was on the screen. *Now.* I pulled Lou down the stairs with me. "Um, Mom?"

"Yes?" she asked, suspicious. Wary.

Lou elbowed me. I took a breath and asked if I could go with Lou and Esme to a wave dance at Roller Gardens.

Eyes narrow, Mom said, "What does that mean, *wave*?'"

"It's just a dance."

Lou piped up. "It's roller skating with music on. At night." I winced. Bad idea to emphasize the after-dark bit. I'd held off asking till Lou was with me, hoping it would help. Fat chance. I was fourteen, but it seemed that with every passing year my parents monitored my movements more closely, as if I were on a backward train away from independence.

Wave dances—essentially a nighttime skating session at the roller rink—were a thing. I loved speed. I relished Saturday afternoons skating around to Joan Jett & the Blackhearts. But I didn't know why "wave dances" were called what they were, or why they were supposedly so great. The plan was to go Friday night. Lou and Esme had talked me into it.

I was the one who'd grown up with Esme—we'd known each other since kindergarten—and I was still getting used to how readily she'd agree to Lou's schemes. When she'd first met Lou, on the bus home the first week of high school, Lou had spent the whole trip telling a joke about a wide-mouthed frog. She'd made it go on and on, with this animal and that animal, giving them all special animal voices, and totally hamming it up when the frog was talking, opening her mouth as wide as she could. *Hi! I'm the wide-mouthed frog. I like to eat flies. What do you like to eat?* Finally, just as the joke's endlessness became unbearable, she veered to the punchline. This entailed the frog speaking through the teeniest mouth possible, to fool a snake whose favourite food was, you guessed it, wide-mouthed frogs. It was so lame I burst out laughing: After all this? Really? That's it? Lou joined in, and then neither of us could stop. Esme looked from her to me and back and said, calmly, "But it wasn't funny." She'd eyed my friendship with Lou skeptically ever since.

Until recently, that is. One night in January we'd all gone to Esme's house to study for our science exam, and Esme had explained to Lou how cells function. She drew pictures on three-ring binder paper and made Lou look at them until she got it. "It's like a choo-choo train," she said. "Here's the whistle. Here's the smoke." She giggled. "Now it's going down the track. Choo-choo!" Someone else might have thought Esme was making fun of them, but Lou was thrilled: suddenly it all made sense. And Esme's guard came down. She still frequently rolled her eyes at Lou, but now she did it in front of her, not just when she and I were alone.

Their connection no longer required me as a link: Lou and Esme were forging their own friendship. I strove to stay in the loop. So here I was, begging permission to go to a dance at the roller rink I wasn't especially interested in. And Mom was far from finished. "Who goes to these things? What sort of people?"

"Normal people. Everybody goes."

"I hate it when you say that. Everybody. Do you think I care what everyone else does?"

What does it cost? What kind of music? What do they have to drink there? How is it chaperoned? How many people do they let in? I tried to monitor my tone, to not sound impatient. The third period of the hockey game was well underway when she turned to Dad and said, "Well, Sandy, what do you think?"

I held my breath and gripped Lou's arm. That was the cue she was giving in.

AS A TODDLER, I FELL OFF THE COUCH—JUMPING ON THE cushions, they tell me—and dinged my head against a corner of the coffee table. That got me two stitches along the upper ridge of the right eyebrow. Eight years later, at softball practice, I misjudged a fly ball. Instead of landing in my open glove, it plunked straight into my forehead. I don't remember falling. When I came to, I was flat on my back on the grass, my teammates staring down at me. A girl said, "Oh my God, the blood!" The ball had pressed the upper rim of my glasses through the skin. It took ten stitches to close the gap, and a long line remained, running straight through the centre of my eyebrow, which had never been delicate or arching, but unruly and thick, and was now split into three—as if to emphasize its width, how much ground it really could cover.

The night of the wave dance I was lying on Lou's candy-striped Ikea futon-sofa bed that opened directly onto the floor and made me think that for her, every night was like camping out. I was telling her about the two scars on my eyebrow, and about the boy named Dino who used to call me "Brow." Very funny. She beckoned me across the room.

She was standing in front of the open closet, still in her school kilt and blouse. She'd been looking for an outfit to change into.

I got up. She started undoing the buttons on her shirt. She pulled one arm out of its sleeve, so her left side was bare. She wore a light beige bra, like me, and, like mine, her breasts were compact, barely there. Her skin was milky white except for a coating of gingery freckles. She twisted her head as if to look over her left shoulder, and then placed a hand beside her neck. "There. Look."

Just behind the shoulder, cut in two by her bra strap, was a patch of smooth, hairless skin, about the size of a fist, a blank spot in the midst of that cascade of freckles. The perimeter was marked by little bumps, and the centre pressed inward, like a piece of cloth had been stretched over a hole and fastened at the edges. "I had a cyst," she said.

I asked her to explain "cyst." She said it was some sort of bump. It didn't hurt, didn't bleed—so why replace it with this?

"They wanted to be on the safe side." Lou pressed down on the spot with her index and middle finger. "Touch it," she said.

The skin felt polished, not like the rest of her shoulder, with its tiny red hairs. It was like a frozen pond in a field, ringed with an uneven bank.

"I can't wear a bathing suit without everyone seeing it. Not even a tank top."

"But it isn't ugly or anything. It's distinctive. Like a tattoo." I had no idea this was the beginning of years of trying, and failing, to convince her this was true.

Skin had been taken from her bum to patch the hole left by the cyst. She screwed up her face when she told me that part. But she had to give me the facts in order to let me in on the joke: the surgeon's name had been Dr. Butt. No kidding. He cut the cyst away and sent it off to the pathologists. Their reports were "inconclusive."

"Inconclusive about what?" I was back on the mattress now, but sitting straight up, alert. She shrugged. She didn't know, or didn't want to say.

All this happened in 1984. Louisa was twelve. This was around the time her parents got divorced, when her father moved out and her mother planned to sell the house. The following summer, she would move to my part of town, and turn up at my bus stop, the first day of grade nine. She started rummaging in a box in the closet. She stood up and handed me a fat book with a hard cover and a pretty script on the front that said *Judy Blume Diary*.

"I wrote about it in here," she said. "You can read it if you want."

"Really?" I took the book and turned the pages.

"There," she said, stopping me. "It's near the end. I haven't written much lately."

June 23, 1984
Dear Diary,

Lots has happened, many things that really affect me! Mom and Dad are separating for good (in my opinion)…We are selling our wonderful house and moving to a townhouse somewhere. What a time. I had that lump removed AGAIN. This time it was really gruesome! Blood everywhere! Blahh! I got stitches too. They are out now. We had our guitar party. We had pizza. It was sooo good!

And, a month later, on a page with her hospital bracelet taped to the edge:

July 19, 1984
Dear Diary,

I got put in the hospital 2 days ago (July 17, 1984). I had a skin graph [sic]. Dr. Butt just told me I had to go in at 4:00 on the 16th. I went in the next morning. When I first heard I cried and cried. Mom sat with me before the operation. But, when they put me on the stretcher I started to cry. I was scared. When they put the needle in the buzzing of the lights got louder and I was gone! When I woke up in the recovery room, I was dizzy. They took me back to my room. I was losing lots of blood, so they told me I had to go back into surgery. But in the end I was fine.

I looked up. Lou was sitting at her desk in front of the rotating makeup mirror, the magnifying side turned toward her. "Most people will never see it," I said.

She swivelled to face me. "It's not most people I care about."

"Well, whoever loves you will have to love your scar. It's part of you." I gave her a solemn look. "Maybe you need to give it a name."

She gasped.

"What? What did I say?"

Her lipstick sailed across the room, a bright pink missile aimed at my head.

I ducked.

THE TEMPERATURE HAD DROPPED TO MINUS TWENTY, and everything had changed. Dad pulled up, and we scrambled shivering into the station wagon. The heater was blasting.

"How was the dance?" my dad asked.

"Fine," I said. "Fun."

"It was *really* fun, Mr. Lahey," said Lou. Esme smacked her thigh. I shot her the warning look, and she raised her eyebrows as if to say, *What? What did I do?*

"Good," said my dad. He pulled out of the parking lot.

I had been dancing with Carlos somewhere in the middle of the rink, the two of us rocking back and forth and side to side, our roller skates clunking. My arms were loose around his neck. His hands were resting on my hips. I turned to face him and my mouth landed right on his lips, which seemed to have been placed just so: right in my path. I thought, "Oh!" and kissed back. In the car, I sat quietly in the front seat, still feeling the kiss, worried that my lips would look as smeared as they felt—that Dad would know. I already couldn't remember the song we'd been dancing to. The kiss had been wet and halting. Just something that had happened involving both of our mouths.

I slowly warmed up. I could feel Lou in the back seat, fit to burst. A few times she nudged the back of my seat with her knee. I turned and glared.

By the time we pulled up outside her place I was wondering: Had it been a dare? Had I been part of some joke? Lou thanked my dad and got out of the car. "Call me," she mouthed through the window.

"Okay!" I said, mimicking her expression. Then I stuck out my tongue. She opened her mouth in mock horror and ran up to the door. My dad pulled away and drove a long block down Lakeshore, the cold air parting for the steaming car, and turned up the street toward Esme's house.

In the morning the phone rang. It was Louisa, of course, calling to talk about Carlos and the kiss. Carlos and the Kiss. It could be the name of a band, or a science fiction novel, in which the kiss transforms the protagonist into a being with permanently puckered lips—or transports him to another civilization, where there's no kissing allowed.

But she didn't ask me about the Kiss.

"You won't believe what happened," she said.

What could have happened in the past ten hours, I thought. We'd come home and slept. Then I'd eaten some Corn Flakes for breakfast while watching a *Scooby-Doo* rerun.

"I got frostbite."

"Frostbite! How?" But as I asked, I flashed back to us driving away as Lou's arm reached out for the door of her house.

"I was locked out."

"Holy crap, Lou. Are you okay?"

By this time both my parents were hovering. I tried to wave them off.

A new lock had been put on the door at Lou's house. She'd forgotten to switch from the old key to the new. It was her brothers' weekend to be at their dad's place, and her mother hadn't come home yet. Lou went into the underground parking lot and got in the car, reasoning it would be warmer down there. She fell asleep. She woke up what seemed like a long time later. She couldn't feel her hands or feet. She went upstairs. Still nobody was home. It was too late to knock on a neighbour's door—and she didn't really know them anyway. So, she went into the little backyard and picked up a lawn chair that was still sitting out from last summer and shook the snow off it. If someone saw her she would just say she was breaking into her own house. That couldn't be against the law, could it? She swung the chair at the kitchen window.

"Lou. Holy shit."

My mother shot me a look. *Language*. I shot one back.

The glass shattered. She pushed the large pieces aside, climbed up on the chair and crawled through the window, cutting her hand. Once inside, she called her uncle, who came over right away. "I won't lose my fingers," she told me. "They're not black."

"Jesus."

"It's okay. I mean, it was scary, but I'm fine."

When I got off the phone and explained what had happened, my father shook his head and pressed down on the back of his neck with his hand.

"She's okay," I said. "It's okay."

He shook his head again.

Once, not long after Louisa and I had met, my mom came home after work and found us in the kitchen, where

Lou was eating croutons right out of the box. They made a loud crunch when she chewed. She loved that we always had a box of croutons in the house. She would tell people at school that she loved coming to my place because you could eat croutons there like chips.

"Tell me, Louisa," my mom began. Uh-oh. What was this? "Do you go to church often?"

Mom, please, no.

"Sometimes," Lou said, looking up at my mother with a fresh handful of croutons on its way to her mouth. "I think about it a lot. I want to believe. I really do. But sometimes I don't, and then I get angry."

I wanted to say, "Excuse me," and yank Louisa into the next room, as though we were in an episode of *Three's Company*. There, in a hoarse whisper, I would say, "Are you crazy? You can't talk like that here!" Instead I stared at the blue, polished floor tiles, waiting for what would happen next.

"Well, you know." Mom's voice was unexpectedly gentle. "I never went to church regularly before I got married."

"You didn't?" This was news to me.

"The Polish church was far away." She straightened. Her voice took on a strained dignity. "In Hamilton. We went on special occasions."

Now it was as though she and Lou were on the same side. Thwarted in spirituality, by factors beyond their control. How had Louisa learned to be so frank? And who knew it would work on my mom? She was now launching into one of her stock stories, about her second date with my father.

"I barely knew him. The car was stopped at a red light. Somewhere in Hamilton, on Barton Street. He turns to me and says, 'What religion are you?'"

Lou's eyes bulged. "Really?"

"The nerve," Mom said.

"It must have been important to him," said Lou, with an air of wisdom and understanding.

"Thank God I answered Catholic." This was Mom's favourite part. "Otherwise I think he would have let me out right there." Her delivery was impeccable. Lou laughed. I'd heard the story a thousand times, but I laughed too.

"He would have," Mom said, "I'm sure of it." Then she grabbed the croutons. "Give me some of those." And she stuck her own hand into the box.

The morning after Louisa was locked out, I saw my father's face crumple. He had failed to watch her step into the house before pulling away. A fourteen-year-old girl— not his own daughter, someone else's. It was late at night, and dangerously cold. She was okay, and not upset with me or with him. I stood before him as these facts were absorbed. I saw him, possibly for the first time, outside our own family circle, at the heart of a series of actions and consequences. I felt the burden of his sense of responsibility, his under- standing of what Lou's mother and uncle must have felt, and what they must now be thinking. The room filled with his regret, and his essential goodness. The tight knot of fear that accompanied my encounters with him loosened, a change that made me aware for the first time that this hard little ball of unease had existed in me at all.

AFTER LOUISA'S SURGERY, BACK AT SCHOOL, EVERYONE came to me for news. One lunch hour I was on the pay phone in the front stairwell, talking to Lou in her hospital room. She was telling me which teachers to approach regarding her missed homework and I was trying to scrib- ble a list in my notebook. It was difficult to stay on track.

Every few seconds someone would come through the doors or down the stairs and see me on the phone. "Is that Lou?" "Are you talking to Louisa?" "Can I say hi?" I would hand the receiver over and lean against the wall beside the bank of phones until they gave it back.

Lou returned home. Her incision, held fast with dissolving stitches—a magical new technology—healed. Weeks passed, during which some scientist somewhere was inspecting the tiny lump that had been cut from beneath her skin. Meanwhile, she now bore a second scar. This new marking, unlike the one that had plagued her all these years, was narrow and short, and tucked discreetly beneath her left arm.

FOUR

Everything's Fine

ONE DAY IN JUNE, HIGH SCHOOL STUDENTS ALL OVER BUR-lington paced the floors of their bedrooms or stood at the front door watching for a figure in that telltale royal-blue Canada Post uniform moving up the laneway. That was me: watching, waiting. It was Lou, as well, I knew. We awaited news of our fate: this was the day university acceptance (or rejection) letters were due to arrive.

Lou called mid-morning. The envelope was fat, so she knew before opening it that the news was good.

"You?"

"Not yet."

"If I got in, you will for sure."

I wasn't worried. Not exactly. It didn't seem possible that we would wind up in different schools, in different cities. I waited until two. Then three. Finally, the package arrived. "We are pleased to inform you…"

I dropped to the living room couch, the letter in my hand, and closed my eyes. "Thank God." I was going to study journalism at Ryerson. It was really going to happen.

We had been talking up Ryerson and its attributes for months, poo-pooing the rival program at Carleton University in Ottawa, where, rumour had it, nobody wrote a real news story—not even a lead for a news story—until second year. At Ryerson, we would be chucked into action immediately. We would earn an "applied" arts degree, which felt like university with teeth. There was a stream to suit us both: broadcast for Lou, magazine for me.

I could see myself walking the campus in downtown Toronto, cutting from the subway stop at Yonge and Dundas over to Victoria, around Lake Devo—a large pond with huge grey rocks rising out of it like toy mountains—to the little brown journalism building on Gould, where I already knew the reporting classes were held in the basement. I'd fallen in love with the place when we'd taken the campus tour. Our guide, in contrast to his tucked-in, preppy counterpart at Western, where we'd been the day before, wore a mangy T-shirt and jeans that looked to have come through the Plague. He high-fived his buddies in the hallways. He let us try out some editing equipment. He warned us about long hours meeting deadlines, and playfully punched a passing professor.

The campus was devoid of Ivy League grandeur. The facilities were like a motley collection of unattractive, sixties- and seventies-era primary and secondary schools jammed together however they could be made to fit. Many of the classrooms were only large enough to hold thirty or so people; the hallways were lined with lockers, like in high school; and the strip clubs on Yonge Street, the head shops and arcades, the labyrinthine Sam the Record Man and the fast-food joints and bargain basements and street people and old men playing chess at stone tables were all part of the package.

Now Louisa and I would be part of it too. I blinked. There was some other news we were still awaiting, from a hospital lab somewhere in Toronto. I hadn't asked Lou about it lately, and she hadn't brought it up. It had been several weeks since her surgery. She'd healed quickly, and the episode had already taken on a fuzzy, memory-like quality. Louisa in the hospital bed, laughing and making no sense, and thanking Esme and me for coming, over and over, was like a scene from another story, one we'd gotten to the end of and closed. I stayed on the couch a little longer, holding my letter. In a minute, I would get up and make my calls, starting with Lou. But not just yet.

DURING OUR GRADUATION MASS LATER THAT MONTH WE sat—girls in white gowns that felt like nurses' uniforms, boys in royal blue like the water rippling in a cool, clean pool—jammed together in pews at the Cathedral Basilica of Christ the King, a tall Gothic structure on a hill overlooking Highway 403 and Burlington Bay. The view included rushing traffic, a drowsy lagoon, the botanical gardens' thick, woodsy havens, and coughing steel-plant smokestacks. Beauty, mystery, and ugliness melded into a sort of intangible force here, a vibration.

Inside the cathedral, it was stifling. As the bishop droned, I looked up to the far-off ceiling, thinking the heat ought to rise, rise, up to the feet of God himself. The waning light filtering through the coloured glass fell upon on the heads of my classmates. I hardly knew either of the students I sat between and resented the alphabetical arrangement. Louisa sat several pews behind, near the witty, sometimes abrasive Cal Perry, who was, I could see—if no one else did—in love with her. His time to act on his feelings was coming to a close. The opportunity would pass him by, as would my own window to make known my crush on my old friend Hal, and as would Lou's to win over Theo, the guy who'd been stringing her along for months, playing I didn't know what sort of game. Soon, we'd all part ways like passengers stepping off a train, forgetting the powerful grip of our nearness to one another.

Though I'd begun to seriously question the Catholic Church's social prejudices and bloody history, I was glad we were marking this moment in solemn fashion. I waited for the offertory hymn, "Be Not Afraid," a stirring song that, to me, had always felt like an almost unholy dare: "You shall cross the barren desert / But you shall not die of thirst." It would be followed by the less ominous Communion hymn, "Here I Am Lord": "I the Lord of sea and sky / I have heard my people cry…" I had a flash memory of Esme and me standing in the front pew of St. Pat's with our fellow members of the paltry youth choir, grasping at the high notes in that gentle, hopeful tune.

Where was Esme? In a pew near the back, in the *S* row. I swung around but couldn't spot her. Was her mother here? She'd finally finished her heavy-duty chemotherapy regimen—she'd lost her hair and felt nauseated and weak for months—and seemed to have improved. But Esme had told me they were talking about more treatment, radiation this time. This wouldn't make her sick like the chemo had, but that was little consolation. Esme's eyes, always so big and round, had shadows beneath them now, which crept up into the corners like a dark vapour.

The bishop's voice swirled in the high archways and bounced against the pillars. I tried to focus. "Ye are the light of the world. A city that is set on a hill cannot be hid." The reading felt eerily familiar. Aha! It was the very verse upon which the musical *Godspell* was based.

A sixties take on Catholicism, *Godspell* made being faithful seem fun—even a little untoward. It'd been staged at our school the previous year, with Lou in the cast and me on the makeup crew. The whole production felt deliciously daring for a Catholic high school: Mary Magdalene's number is exceedingly sultry, and all the characters' instinctive response to feeling joyous is to drink wine. I'd often sat with Lou while she practised the chorus number, "Light of the World," as well as her solo piece, the more difficult "Day by Day." These songs were somewhere inside me, as entrenched as those old hymns.

Watch out, I read between the lines as the bishop drew the words from the page and poured them into the thick warm air of the cathedral. *You've been given this one life. Don't squirrel it away. Squander it. Light it. Use it up.*

WITH ONE HAND ON THE RAILING AND THE OTHER pressed against the wall, I teetered up a carpeted staircase, stepping into the soft fibres between tuxedo pant legs and pantyhose-smooth knees. I'd long ago lost my drink and my date.

"Has anyone seen Lou?" Bleary faces shook in response. "Are you sure? I really have to find her."

These were my classmates, cradling beer bottles or plastic cups of cola-rum mixes, teetering, their contents sloshing toward the brims. The girls wore shiny, strapless gowns, in taffeta or faux silk. Some had crushed corsages pinned to their chests. I had taken mine off, an orchid, and left it somewhere.

"You have to keep it," Lou had said.

"What will I do with it?"

"Press it in a book." Her slender hands had opened as if to say, it's obvious. She wore a shimmering forest-green dress that gathered in folds and swooped over one shoulder, neatly hiding her scar. Her bare arms looked smooth and pale, with a sprinkling of freckles like a dusting of cinnamon. She was sitting on a step next to James, her date. Their hips mashed together as they pressed to one side of the stairs to let people get by. His hand rested on the slippery green fabric above her knee.

"A special book," she said. "A favourite book."

"Wait, I know!" James grinned. "*Anne of Green Gables*."

"Shut up."

"What? It's funny. That's funny, right Lou?" He was leaning into her bare arm, his face tipping forward toward her small breasts, which were amplified by the folds of the dress.

That was hours ago. Now the two of them were nowhere to be seen. I'd laughed when Lou said she wanted to ask James to be her date for grad. Then, when I saw she was serious, I said, "You can't. He's a monster. He's completely amoral." She said she didn't care: he was cute, he was funny. He was way less intense than her old boyfriend, Jeffrey. I'd been so happy when, after the surgery, she'd finally broken up with him. First of all, Jeffrey forgot all about her surgery and called to ask why he hadn't heard from her all week. Then he apologized so extravagantly she became annoyed. "I'm so selfish," he said. "Yes," she agreed, "you can be." Second, he came home to visit—he was already in university—and gave her the sex ultimatum. "I've waited all year," he said. "I go to school with grown-ups. If you're not ready I'm going to have to move on." She told him to go ahead and move on, and I told her I was proud.

The same week, walking home from the bus, James had started raving about this new show called *The Simpsons*.

"It's a cartoon, but it's not for kids."

We gave him our skeptical look and he said seriously, it's hilarious, cross my heart, hope to die, and all that crap. "It's on in twenty. Come over. I'll prove it to you."

He lived around the corner from me. Fine, okay. We walked over to his place and descended into the basement family room that was a familiar fixture in all of our homes. He flopped on the couch, flicked on the TV and, voila! There was Lisa and her saxophone. Marge's hair! Wonky, unmerciful humour. While the three of us sat laughing, Louisa turned away from the TV to look at James in profile. Her hair was pulled back into a crooked French twist, and I could see the thoughts twisting through her mind. *Jeffrey would have no time for* The Simpsons. *He'd scorn it. Compared to James, Jeffrey was a pill. And James is kind of cute. His freckles are lighter than mine, but he has so many.* I nudged her, just to get her to look away. "What?" she said, her mouth open, her eyes questioning. I said, "It's funny, isn't it, the show?"

I'd known James since kindergarten. At some point we'd gotten in the habit of walking to catch the school bus together. He told me stories about the girls he went after, how he sweet-talked them, and the ones he never bothered to call back. I loved having a guy in my life who said things straight up. He was funny. He was my friend. But I didn't want him messing with Lou. And now the two of them had disappeared somewhere in this house full of drunk teenagers. I had to find them.

"Hey, I'm looking for Louisa." People ignored me, noses in their drinks. I stumbled up the next crowded staircase. I heard Esme, her marvellous ringing laugh echoing down as if from a far-off church tower. She was in a little group by the window, a drink in her hand. Her dress was peach and form-fitting, with a mild, tasteful ruffle around her waist. Adam stood at her side, his hair short and spiky, his tuxedo jacket pulled off and a red cummerbund around his waist, glinting like a troubadour's cape.

Esme would understand. I moved toward her, as if toward a life raft, bouncing between partiers, tossed by waves. Look at her there in those heels, so tall, so steady! I'd kicked off my own shoes and was marching around in the black hose I'd bought, which came in one of those plastic eggs at the drugstore. I'd worn holes into both heels. I moved forward. I was almost there. I reached for Esme's arm. I stumbled. She giggled.

"Anita! You're drunk."

I shook my head. That wasn't the point. I tugged her toward me. I leaned in. I whispered. "I have to find Lou. She's going to have sex with James. We have to stop her."

Esme took my arm. "No!" She veered. I veered. "Are you sure?" We gripped each other. "It's a hunch." We were swimmers going down. "Ever since Jeffrey. It's like she has to prove something." Then we regained balance. Something held us. Adam was propping us between his arms, grinning. His beer bottle tipped and dribbled onto my neck.

"Sorry," he said, and reached back and tried to wipe it off. We were listing again.

"Whoa," I said.

"Whoa!" Esme said.

Then we were still, the three of us, floating in a huddle like you would after you've capsized, to keep warm. Our foreheads were touching. Adam spoke. I felt his breath on my nose. "What's all this about Louisa? Good for her. She should have some fun."

Esme broke the huddle. "Let's go find her." She bent down and adjusted a shoe. Then she stood up, straight as ever. She turned to Adam. She waved a hand at him, like a housewife in full control of her domain. "Entertain yourself. Just keep doing what you're doing."

We went up and down, room by room. It was an older house, with ivy crawling up the bricks outside. Inside, it was like a rabbit warren: hallways, landings, staircases, doors. I thought of *The Lion, the Witch and the Wardrobe*. Lou had snuck through the magic portal and was now beyond reach, losing her virginity with James, of all people.

"Hurry," I said to Esme. She had her head stuck in the downstairs bathroom. She was pulling back the shower curtain.

"I'm just making sure. That Louisa's crafty, you know."

I started telling everyone we passed that if they saw Lou they were to tell her Anita said she wasn't allowed to have sex with James. Absolutely forbidden. "It's a bad idea. She'll regret it."

Then Esme was gone too and Will, my date, had me in his arms. "I've been looking all over for you," he said. We were by the back door, which was open to the garden. People were sitting on damp grass and lawn chairs, crumpled in their formal wear. The sky was a light grey with a pale pink blush along its base. "I'm looking for Lou," I told him. "She's in trouble."

Will had dark hair, lively eyes. He could slow them down to serious and pensive, and he did so now. "What do you mean? Can I help?"

I shook my head. "It's been ages since I've seen her." I slumped onto the stone step. It was too late. We were still waiting for the analysis of the lump—that rogue piece of her they'd shipped to a lab somewhere. The process was so far beyond my comprehension I didn't even know what to wonder, let alone what to ask. How would the lump be analyzed? Dropped in some magic chemical solution that isolated all its parts? Now and then I'd bring it up, or Lou would say, out of the blue, "No news. Good or bad?" Will sat down and pulled me close. I closed my eyes. I nuzzled my head into the hollow between his shoulder and his jaw.

"Lou's a smart girl," he said. "She can take care of herself."

"I don't know," I said. I pulled back to face him. "She's getting away from me. We're getting so old."

"She's just doing what she has to do. She's your best pal. That won't change."

"How did you get to know so much? How did you get to be such a good guy?" He shrugged and his head tipped forward again. I pressed a knuckle lightly under his chin and lifted. "I'm sorry I disappeared."

"It's okay," he said. He lifted his beer. "I had compensation." He tilted the bottle toward me. I took it and drank. The beer was warm and syrupy.

"Ew." I handed it back. "How long have you been carrying that around?"

"I'm not a guzzling man," he said.

I took the bottle from him and put it on the ground. I slid a finger over his lower lip. It was red like the skin of an apple, and amazingly soft.

"What is it?" he said. "Why are you so sad?"

I shook my head. I placed a hand on either side of his face and pulled him toward me.

A GRAVELLY *AHEM, AHEM*. A THROAT WAS BEING CLEARED. Something pressed into my calf. Toes.

"Anita, Anita!"

"We leave you alone and look what happens. Naughty, naughty girl."

We pulled apart. Will smiled and looked down. *Come back here*, I thought. But I turned to the voices.

Louisa and James were standing before the step, grinning, not holding hands or even touching. Their faces were hard to make out in the sun, overexposed.

"Lou!" I jumped up. "I've been looking all over for you."

"I can see that." She caught James's eye. He chuckled.

"She was," said Will. "I'm her witness."

"Esme and I were on this massive hunt for, like, half the night—"

"We just went for a walk. It was so beautiful to be out while the sun was coming up."

She held the skirt of her dress up in her right hand, as though she'd just walked over a puddle. Her hair was still pulled back in the pretty combs she'd bought. Wispy strands fell loose around her face, gingery in the light. She was dishevelled, but no more than I was.

"You watched the sun rise. You two. Together." I looked from her to James and back.

"Uh-huh." Lou grinned.

"That sounds pretty romantic," said Will, who was now sprawled on the step, shielding his eyes as he looked up at them.

"Let's not get carried away," said James. "It's the sun. It happens every day."

The morning sunlight settled around Lou like a new mood: contentment. The tension that had been building around her all year had lifted. Had she slept with James in some shadowy corner of the yard? Why had I been so fixated on this? Probably he'd just made her laugh. Good thing she spent the night with him and not with me.

Lou held up a paper bag. "We got breakfast."

I took Will's hand and pulled him up and we followed Louisa and James out into the dewy grass.

JULY ABSORBED US IN ITS LANGUID HUMIDITY, THOSE eternal longings for patches of shade. Two years before, Lou and I had gotten gigs as day camp counsellors. We were seasoned at the job now, working at sites in different parts of town, caught up in planning crafts, games, and songs that would keep twenty to thirty kids happily occupied for hours. In the evenings we'd meet with fellow counsellors in someone's backyard, or at a bar, sit back, let our sticky arms fall away from our bodies, and vent. It was impossible to avoid "bad" campers—we all had them. The ones who threw clumps of homemade playdough at the gym ceiling when we were stuck indoors on rainy days. The overly rambunctious ones who turned dodgeball into a full contact sport. The smarmy eleven-year-olds who taunted, and sometimes straight-out corrupted, our leaders-in-training, some of whom were barely older than the campers themselves.

There were twenty-two "campsites" at designated school grounds scattered about the city. Some were essentially weedy soccer fields with maybe a single scraggly tree off to one side. This year, I was lucky. I was assigned to a school with a small forest and creek at the far end of the field. My partner was competent—unlike last summer, when I had to organize everything myself—and easy-going. At 7:30 a.m. each day I biked to work, lunch in my pack. Campers were dropped off at eight.

By this, my third summer on the job, I was a solid counsellor. I had tried-and-tested tricks. I knew how to plan. My campers generally liked me. But Louisa's *loved* her. She had a knack for goofiness and—it was innate or honed from years of drama classes—she could think on the spot. If an activity was flopping before her eyes, the kids growing restless, she'd reroute. Like that. Snap. Every week we had a field trip: we'd get on the bus and converge at the pool, say, with all the other camps in town. That's when I'd see Lou in action, leading her happy charges through rousing songs or crafts-on-the-go, while I was busy just trying not to lose a kid—or three. At school, though Louisa was a good student, I'd been the one who sailed through. I almost never got a mark lower than an A, whereas, in some subjects, Louisa struggled. (She once got so frustrated in math she wrote a poem sarcastically titled "Ode to Finite" and showed it to her teacher, which won her some sympathy, and some extra help.) But here at camp, outside what was, for me, the safety of the classroom, it was Lou who excelled. I was glad we weren't partnered up. Then I'd have spent every day comparing my performance to hers—and coming up short.

My favourite camper that summer was an eight-year-old named Maurice who was blessed with cleverness, a well-placed cowlick, and a seemingly bottomless well of enthusiasm. Everyone, at least once a summer, had a Maurice: the kind of soulful, good-natured kid who instills in camp counsellors everywhere that glowy, gushy feeling that gets us teary over late-night beers. Camp was a separate world you sank into, a place to belong—and we'd get fierce and emotional about that belonging. But this was, let's be honest, merely a day camp—no cabins, no lake— and I did feel relief when 4 p.m. rolled around each afternoon and the parents turned up. I'd watch them carting off their kids and think to myself: these poor people don't get any time to themselves. The only child I was sorry to see walk away, his hand in his mom's, was Maurice.

The weeks passed. August's pleasant daze rolled in, the mornings cooled, and after breakfast I'd throw on a green hoodie with S.A.C. printed on its back, for Summer Activity Centres. By mid-morning the sun would be strong again, and I'd peel it off. Then, suddenly, as if we'd woken from a dream, camp was over. Our camp day sheets were supplanted by to-do lists. We had supplies and clothes to buy, budgets to pore over. We were on the verge of moving away from home.

Lou had stopped mentioning the pathology report. I'd quit asking. Some nights we'd drive the streets of Burlington with a tape in, the car humming as we passed through pools of artificial light. It was, I suppose, a kind of farewell. After 11 p.m., somewhere around the third or fourth run-through of "Fast Car," I suggested we pull into Tim Hortons. Lou was still enthralled, but I was sick of Tracy Chapman. I got a coffee with milk and an apple fritter; Louisa, hot chocolate and a honey cruller. She hated coffee—it was too bitter. We carried our mugs and plates to one of the little metal tables that had seats bolted on.

Lou looked at me over the rim of her steaming mug. Her eyes were often startling. Neat, thin eyebrows arched over blue pools, a dark storm-water blue.

"I had a weird dream."

"Oh, yeah?" I sipped my coffee, wondering what I was in for.

There'd been the dream she and her brother had "shared": they'd both wound up on the landing in the middle of the night, looking for his flip book. Who knew what to make of that? Then there was the more conventional one about being stuck naked in an elevator. In Lou's case, the doors opened to the gymnast she'd loved since grade nine. When he saw her he said, "Louisa, that's no way to prepare for the uneven bars." For weeks after that, if she saw him coming down the hall, she would whisper furiously, "Hide me!" She was worried that maybe he'd had the dream too, the same one at the same time, like what had happened with her and Jon.

"If so, he saw *the dream you* naked."

"But he would have known it was me, and he'd think that's how I look."

"But you said he didn't really look anyway."

"I know. That's what's so awful. Am I that unattractive?"

Lou tore off a piece of cruller and dipped it in her hot chocolate. "Grandfather Jon." That was her brother's namesake. He'd died when Louisa's mother was a little girl. Of Hodgkin's lymphoma. Cancer. She popped the soggy dough into her mouth.

"What about him?"

"He was in the dream."

"Oh. How do you know it was him?" They'd obviously never met.

"Pictures."

"Right, of course. Was he old or young?"

"He never got old, really. He was only in his forties when he died. He was upset."

"In your dream? Maybe that's what happens when you die too young. You feel cheated."

"That's awful."

"I'm sorry. It's just—don't they say ghosts are unsettled souls?"

"It wasn't like that. He wasn't a ghost. He was wearing overalls. He was walking down a long corridor, and he kept turning back and trying to stop me."

"From…"

"Following him."

"Um. Right. And this was what kind of corridor?"

"I don't know. White, maybe. It was dark in the hallway but there was daylight outside. And there was a window at the end. I could see it. I was thinking there was something to see out the window."

I spun my coffee cup around and watched the liquid inside jostle about. "Louisa, that's creepy. The tunnel? The light?"

She picked at her cruller, tearing off sugary strands. "He was so angry. But I didn't listen. I kept following him."

"Did he talk to you?"

She nodded. "'Your mother,' he kept saying. 'Just think of her.' Then I stopped, and he stopped, and I shouted, 'You left her. It was you!' And then he disappeared." She twirled some hair around her finger, then let it go. "Then I was standing outside, and there was all this traffic and I didn't know which way to walk, and I wished I was back inside the hallway with Grandpa Jon. And then I woke up."

"It's because you're thinking about Esme and her mom."

"Maybe."

We sat a little while longer with our mugs. Two old men were chatting at the table next to us. One of them smiled and doffed his Blue Jays cap in a kind, grandfatherly way. Tufts of grey hair stuck out below the mesh of the cap over his ears. We probably looked very young to him. He was maybe wondering what we were doing out so late. But I didn't feel young. I had a vague memory of endless, hot, humid, summer days, days when I'd finished with all my library books and felt almost painfully lethargic, incapable of action. That never happened now. Now the days were like dominoes falling into one another: just as I got my footing I started tipping forward, into the next day. And then there was this haunting, chilling premonition. It was nothing, it was a dream, but it ushered in a mood, an emotional weather system that clung to me like a mist; it followed me through the motions of the daytime, the way Lou had followed Grandfather Jon down that corridor.

AT LONG LAST, IT CAME. LOUISA CALLED TO SHARE THE news. The lump had contained, apparently, two abnormal cells.

"Iffy," she told me.

"Iffy? What does that mean?"

"I don't know. They weren't normal."

"But they're gone."

"Yeah."

"Two cells. Wow. That's microscopic."

"I know."

I was on my usual kitchen chair, back to the wall beneath where the black phone hung. The same place I'd been the day she'd told me about the lump in the first place. The same pose. Except it was daytime now, and two seasons had passed. Summer was seeping away, sinking down into the dry lawns and creek beds. All the proper cycles were in place.

I had been waiting and waiting for a certain word to be used, but it never was.

Part Two

FIVE

Who, What, Where, When, Why

THE PILLS SAT IN SLOTS IN A LITTLE PLASTIC DISC, ONE for each day. They were pink and circular and barely larger than crumbs. They came with a fake velvet satchel, also pink, in which to keep the disc. The microfilm, we called it.

"Sshh. I have ze microfilm in my purse."

"It is ze great secret. No one must know!"

"Shshsh!"

"Shsh!!"

I turned the disc one notch and gingerly tipped the pill for Sunday into my hand. "Jesus. What if I drop it?" That would be just like me.

Lou held one in her palm, at a distance. "How am I going to swallow this?"

I laughed.

"I'm not joking. I have a thing." She was watching the pill as though it might jump. "I can't get them down. They— they stick in my throat."

In all these years, how had I missed this phobia? Luckily, she hadn't *really* been sick when she'd found that lump—luckily no one had made her take medicine.

"Lou, it's, like, one-tenth of a Smartie. It's like swallowing nothing."

Indeed, the birth control pills were so small that it was difficult to imagine each one could truly be as important as the doctor in the university health clinic had claimed. Three months, he'd told us. You must take one at the same time every day for three months before you can be sure.

Three months! Louisa and I had sat side by side facing him, her red hair spilling over her shoulders a dramatic addition to the white-walled examination room. She appeared as alarmed as I felt. "What about before that?" Three months would take us well into December, a lifetime away. I imagined Simon's face, hearing this.

Simon was my new boyfriend. He was also one of our roommates. In fact, his room was directly next to Lou's and mine. Our co-op was divided into units, like small apartments, housing six tenants who shared a kitchen, common room, and couple of bathrooms. I was studiously ignoring the obvious fact that, should something go terribly wrong between Simon and me, we'd still be sharing a toilet, tub, and fridge.

The doctor, boyish and cute—he seemed barely out of his twenties—had brought in an extra chair because we'd said we might as well talk to him together, there was no reason not to. He shrugged. "You need to double up," he said.

"You mean . . ."

"Condoms. Spermicidal gels. Whatever you're comfortable with. But something."

"What a drag," I said.

He laughed. "Look, it's a low dose that I'm suggesting. If you want something stronger—"

"No, thank you," Lou said.

"Ditto," I said.

"Well, as I explained, it needs time to build up in your system."

"Yeah, we know. You said that."

He looked from me to Lou and back, and, for a moment, seemed trapped. He was leaning back, slouching, his elbows on the clean white counter, his white smock open to reveal a plaid button-down shirt and jeans. This was a surprise: a doctor in jeans. He was just a guy, after all. He shifted and straightened, succeeding in making himself taller.

"Got it?"

We nodded. You could almost hear us gulp.

Now we stood in our digs at our student co-op, a prescription each stuffed into our wallets. We were trying to figure out how we—who were not even capable of keeping our room remotely tidy—would remember to take this stupid pill at the same time every day.

"It would help if we had a routine."

"Who are we kidding? We'll never stick to it."

"We'll have to."

In Lou's blue eyes shone a hint of the fierceness that always emerged when she was inspired to improve herself. The time we were going to jog every morning all summer, say. That plan lasted two days, as Esme still liked to remind us.

"Yeah," she said, a familiar conviction rising. "We'll get up at the same time every day. And take it with breakfast."

"That means having breakfast."

"See? This will be good."

"It's so typical that it's the girl who has to worry about this. What do *they* have to worry about?"

Lou shrugged. "Would you want it to be up to them?"

"Good point."

"Can you imagine? Would you trust Simon to remember?"

"No fucking way. Absolutely not." I considered. "Glen might manage, though."

"I suppose. He could take it with his Slurpee."

We laughed. When Louisa's boyfriend, Glen, had moved to Toronto from Vancouver that fall, the first thing he'd done was go hunting for the nearest 7-Elevens, so he could compare the quality of their Slurpee machines.

"But what if he couldn't find a 7-Eleven? Then you'd be screwed."

"Yeah. I know." A pause, our eyes met, laughter. That, of course, was the point.

Now, as she continued to stare at the pill in her hand, I asked her, "What did you do when you were a kid and you had to take something?"

"I crushed it."

"Well?"

I coaxed her down the hall to the kitchen. We got out two spoons, a glass, and the jug of orange juice. She filled the glass with juice, then picked up a spoon and placed the pill in its silvery hollow. She reached out her empty hand.

I handed her the other spoon. She leaned over the counter and pressed the second spoon into the first. I watched, expecting the tiny pill to pop out from between them, bounce off a wall, and disappear behind the stove. But I heard crackling instead, as she ground it slowly into a powder. She held up the spoon, and we saw that the inside of the pill was white, and cakey. "Do you think they use food colouring?"

"God knows."

"Why does it have to be pink anyway? Why couldn't they give us a good strong colour? Why not red? Why not something dramatic? Why not black?"

"It's not political."

"Of *course* it's political. Pink. Girls. I hate that crap."

"I know."

She sighed. "Anyway, black is the absence of colour."

"Yeah. I've never understood that. What does that really mean? The *absence* of colour." When I recall conversations like this I think, man, I must have been draining sometimes. Did I have to question *everything*? Could I let nothing go?

In grade ten, Lou and I had sat together in science—the very place we'd have learned that black is actually the absence of *light*. It appears to have no colour because it absorbs every bit of light that hits it, leaving only darkness. I still struggle to fully understand this. The light is in there, somewhere—so why can we no longer see it? It has to do with the makeup of molecules in the substance—does the light bounce off or sink in? At what trajectory? You could explain all this and more, all the way to the outer limits of scientific knowledge on the colour black, and still I'd be thinking, "Okay, sure, but *why*?" And Lou would want me to just move on. "You look good in black, you know," she might say, by way of distraction. "You should wear it more often."

Once, in the middle of our science teacher's spiel on the atom, Louisa passed back a sheet of lined, three-ring binder paper full of her big, round handwriting. "We had to write a profile for English," she whispered. "I did you." I laid the sheet over my notebook and began to read, knowing this would mean I'd struggle over whatever homework was coming our way. A profile? Of me? I had, she'd written, chestnut-brown hair, and "an interestingly pretty face, not like another." I was "kind, sensitive, and very sincere," and my best quality was that I was "enthusiastic and optimistic even when the world was falling in" around me. I couldn't believe she'd written all this about me, especially when she wrote that she felt like she'd known me all her life. Then I got to the end. "Anita's only negative quality is her stubbornness. When she sets her mind to something, she does it, regardless. It's not that she hurts other's feelings. It is just that it can really get on your nerves."

Stubborn? Annoying? Huh? Someone pushed against my chair. Hot breath on my ear, the low rumble of a guy's voice, too close. "What are you, lezzies?"

I knew him. One of those guys who'd slouch on a chair with arms crossed and legs spread wide, wearing a scowl that said none of this was worth his time. He'd been skimming Lou's paper over my shoulder. "Get lost." I pushed my elbow into his side, hating to make contact with him at all. The teacher asked if everything was all right over there. I straightened and said, "Yes, fine." When I got the chance I mouthed "Thank you" to Lou. But I wasn't sure I meant it.

Now, in our co-op kitchen, Lou gasped. "Careful!"

I had picked up the glass of juice and was pouring it into the spoon while she held it steady. It had nearly overflowed. I straightened the glass and stepped back. The liquid bubbled up, and on the surface sat white flecks of the drug. Wincing, she plugged her nose, tipped her head back, and opened her mouth. Slowly, slowly, she raised the spoon—I cringed, afraid the spoon would wobble, the juice would spill, and the pill would be lost.

But in it went. She slid the spoon back out between her lips, hesitated, and swallowed. Then she dropped the spoon, grabbed the glass, and took a giant gulp of juice. She sat down, breathing as though she'd just run to catch a bus. "Only eighty-nine days to go."

I put the jug back in the fridge.

IT WAS NO USE. I SAT ON MY BED, MY TYPEWRITER IN MY lap and scrawled papers spread over the mattress. Unworkable leads. Lists of facts. Blocks of data in different shades of ink—red and orange, blue and green. How to make something from the notes I'd taken all week at inquest court? What was the story, really? The apparent neglect of the landlords, who had failed to keep the smoke detectors in working order? The poor condition of the rooming house that had burned down? The fact that those living in poverty were more likely to suffer catastrophes, and less likely to have the insurance that would help them through? None of this was new. None of it was the crux of the matter.

It was January. I'd been writing an article a week since September. You'd think I'd have figured out by now how to do it.

"Fuck it." I slid my typewriter off my lap and said to Lou, "A break? I'll make tea."

Louisa shook her head, barely turning her head to answer. She sat at her desk, facing the wall, hunched over and writing. "I've got some already, thanks." She nodded at the little white pot on her desk. It was round and sturdy. A curl of steam rose from its angled spout.

The teapot. Right. Her Christmas present from Glen: a tiny pot that sat in its own wide mug, designed for single servings. You steeped the tea, then lifted the pot out of the mug and poured. I knew she treasured this pot because it was a gift from Glen. But once she'd begun to use it, our own tea ritual, which had become one of my favourite parts of our new domestic arrangement, fell away.

Four months had passed since Labour Day weekend, when my dad had ferried us and our boxes of clothes into the city in the company van. Nobody spoke much on the drive. Lou had been teary when we picked her up: she felt she was abandoning her mother. I, however, was so anxious to escape home that I felt guilty. I kept trying to catch Lou's eye. I wanted that familiar thrill to ripple between us: as of tonight, we'd have our own place, away from our families, away from Burlington. We'd been planning this for so long. Was it really upon us? But she was far away. Our other friends had warned us repeatedly against living together. "What if you end up hating each other?" Esme had asked, only the other night, over take-out burgers. We'd ignored her. Anyway, we didn't have the luxury for such worries: we'd done the math, we were too poor to live apart.

We'd signed on at a twenty-two-storey student co-op just off campus, a place famous for its parties and its two-decades-old layers of grime. It was founded in the late 1960s so that students attending Ryerson—the school had no residence back then—would have somewhere affordable to live near campus. The building was a short walk south of Toronto's gay village and en route east from Yonge Street to Cabbagetown, that jumbly neighbourhood where rooming houses cowered next to carefully refurbished, peak-roofed Victorians. The co-op was a tenant-owned and tenant-operated dwelling, a nice idea that only half worked in a building inhabited by undergraduates, who couldn't care less what the place would look like after they were gone, never mind who'd mop up the puke in the elevator on any given morning.

Not that we knew any of that yet. So far, our knowledge was purely practical. It cost $220 each per month for a giant double room, as opposed to $280 for a tiny single. We'd decided to share a room and save the money.

It was a clear, bright day, and we took the curves and hills of the Gardiner Expressway at a clip, catching that one dip in the pavement west of the CNE grounds that made your stomach flop. I nudged Lou and pointed out the window to the big red letters atop the Royal York Hotel. She half-grinned. I was caught by the city's incredible heft. Light glazed the tinted bank towers and reflected back over the clustered downtown buildings, and gave all the concrete and stone and glass a soft glow that was like a warm welcome, like the whole city was watching us arrive and whispering: *here you are, we've been waiting, come in, please, make yourselves at home.*

It was deep winter now, and our arrival back on that warm September weekend already seemed a memory from a former life. Dingy as the place was, I loved life at the co-op, including the independence I'd gained, and that Lou was part of the package. Five years into our friendship, our companionship felt natural and homey, and our conversations—from those focused on our grocery list to those about life, the future, and everything—really just part of one big one that never truly ended. Even on cold nights, we'd sit with our steaming mugs of tea on the wide ledge inside our fifth-floor window. We'd peer down at the smattering of prostitutes pacing the sidewalk in their platform shoes and faux-fur jackets. They carried cell phones the size of lap dogs. These were the days when many people had begun to buy car phones. My dad had one he used for work, a weighty contraption set on the console between the front seats. The women below our window were the first people we'd seen walking down the street with phones held up to their ears, actual phones. Their voices rose, temptingly clear, into earshot. "Uh-huh, I know, don't I know it." "It's a cold one tonight." The halves of conversations that we heard were disappointingly banal, yet we listened hard, anxious to glean some clue to these women who, though they stood right below our window, lived lives we could scarcely imagine.

Tonight, though, Lou wasn't interested in my company. Sitting in the window alone while she sat at her desk with her back to me was unappealing. I decided to take my tea break in the common room. As I crossed our room toward the door, Lou shifted in her chair, and I caught sight of a familiar blue cover. This wasn't homework. It was her journal.

God, I thought. *Not again.*

Glen.

WE'D BEEN LIVING IN TORONTO LESS THAN A WEEK AND had come to see a band perform in the Hub, a cavernous campus cafeteria that was transformed into a pub on Thursday nights. Amid a throng of drunk and half-drunk students, we furiously tried to step dance, jumping and slamming our heels and toes into the floor, laughing uproariously and throwing our arms sloppily about. Oh, the bliss of not caring, of just tossing your body on the music like a bauble on the sea.

Lou elbowed me, and covertly directed my gaze to the fringe of the dance floor.

"He's the one."

I rolled my eyes. She was always making these grand declarations. "You're being melodramatic."

"Anita. Look at him."

"I am." He was tall, and dressed in jeans and a long black overcoat, his hands stuffed in the pockets. His dark hair was loosely blow-dried, a little longer in the back—very Bryan Ferry. Or Paul Young. I shrugged. "He looks pretentious."

The music picked up again, a raucous, jig-like tune, fiddles racing, and Mika, one of our roommates, pulled us out of our huddle. "Come on, girls!"

Pretentious, I repeated to Lou, making a face.

No way, she said. But then I noticed our roommate Simon—also on the fringe of the dance floor, where the boys often are. He was looking our way. My way.

Simon had moved in a couple of days after us, so by the time he arrived, we were pretty much set up. Lou's bright yellow comforter was laid out on her bed. Her copies of *The Outsiders*, *The Glass Menagerie*, and *Anne of Green Gables* lined the metal shelf above her desk, alongside a volume of Greek myths and a pocket dictionary. I had *Little Women*, *The Chrysalids*, Timothy Findley's *The Wars*, and George Bernard Shaw's *Joan of Arc*. I'd dangled a summer camp dream catcher off the shelf, and our big tie-dyed S.A.C. flag was tacked to the wall. The walls were still drab, and the floor tiles the colour of grey dishwater, but the sun was streaming in our big, open window, casting a pattern of the screen on the floor, over a corner of Lou's comforter and partway up the wall. It was starting to feel like home.

I grabbed the chalkboard off a pile of things on my bed. "Here, help me with this." I held it up against the wall by the doorframe. "Here?"

"Yeah. That might work."

We had plans for the chalkboard. During our last year of high school, we'd gotten in the habit of recording memorable quotes. We thought it would be fun to write a good quote up on the wall until something more interesting came along. We'd keep a record of the erased quotes in a notebook. I turned to Lou. "What will we hang it with?"

"I'll give you a nail."

That wasn't Lou. It was a male voice. In the doorway. We turned. He was fair and tall and had a friendly smile. I remember he barely fit under the doorframe.

"Hi," Lou said.

"Wow," he said. "You're like, making the room look good. You've already done more than I did to my room all last year. I'll give you all the nails you want. And a hammer. You girls should really have a hammer. Don't leave home without one."

"We didn't think of that."

"First year, eh?" He was in second-year RTA.

"What's that?"

"Radio and Television Arts." That was Lou answering me. "I was thinking about it myself—maybe I should have done that instead of journalism."

"It's a good program," the guy said.

"You're already doubting?" I said.

"It crossed my mind."

"Way more fun than journalism," he said.

"Hmm." I felt ganged up on. But also intrigued. His name was Simon. He had what sounded like a watered-down Australian drawl, which was oddly appealing. "Where are you from?" I asked, thinking he would tell us somewhere over an ocean.

"Burlington."

"No way! So are we. But why do you—"

"Talk funny?" He shrugged. "It's just how I talk."

He looked embarrassed. I wanted to fix it. "It's kind of cool. You could pretend you were from somewhere else." There was a pause, and our eyes met. I looked away and resumed my unpacking. As soon as he was gone Lou cleared her throat.

"What?"

"Oh. Nothing."

That was just a few days before, but dancing with Lou in the Hub, I reflected that it already felt completely normal to be sharing digs with Simon and our other roommates. These included Casey, who had locks of long dark hair, played guitar, and was still devoted to his high school girlfriend; Mika, who was a year ahead and adopted a kind, mothering way with Lou and me; and Troy, who watched two episodes of *Star Trek* a day, sometimes three, while eating a burger and fries from the sketchy burger joint nearby called Harvey's, where the sex workers who worked our block sometimes ate. "Hooker Harvey's," he'd informed us. Troy had this street-savvy way about him, though he seemed to rarely go out. My intense fondness for them all seemed out of whack with the short time in which I'd known them: close quarters shifted you past the acquaintance phase in a hurry.

During our next break from dancing, Lou's guy introduced himself. Glen Mackay of Vancouver. He was in journalism too. That was all I learned that night, because Simon had also wandered over. He leaned in close—the music was loud—and said, "I noticed *The Chrysalids* on your bookshelf. I love that book." I told him I'd refused to give it back after we read it for English class.

"You stole it?"

"No, I pretended I lost it. I had to pay for it."

Our noses were nearly touching. We wandered away from Lou and Glen.

"Is this a good idea?" Lou asked, when we were crawling into bed that night half-drunk.

"What do you mean?"

"Well, you live in the same unit. You hardly know him. What if—"

"Ssh!" I said. "What if he can hear?"

"That's what I mean." She was whispering, leaning over the edge of her bed toward me.

"I think it'll be okay. I'm not worried."

"It'll be hard for him to sneak around on you."

"True."

"You'll see each other at your worst—no surprises."

"Nope."

"Easy access!"

"Shut up." I reached up and switched off the lamp over my desk.

LATER THAT WEEK THE FOUR OF US WENT TO THE HARD
Rock Cafe at the SkyDome. Glen had never gone out for
wings; apparently it wasn't a West Coast thing. There was no
game on. We sat by the window looking out on the empty
stadium, thousands of unoccupied chairs encircling the lit
field, an eerie sight. When the platter arrived heaped with
wings, all smothered in honey-mustard sauce, Glen regarded
them warily.

"So," he said. "These are the wings, eh? There must be a
couple dozen chickens here." Then he shook his head and
said, "Forget it," as though he was sorry to put us through it.
He picked up a tiny wet-nap and feigned slipping it surreptitiously into his wallet, a stunt that elicited groans all
around the table.

I gave Lou a meaningful look. "Say it," I said. "You know
you want to."

She bit into a wing. "These are really good."

"I'm afraid of them," said Glen.

"Say what?" asked Simon. He leaned forward. He had a
curious nature. I liked that. That afternoon we'd lain side
by side on his bed, reading. If you can count reading the
same paragraph over and over as reading. When I could
stand it no longer I let my book close over my thumb and
turned to face him, his clean jaw line, the inviting indent
behind his ear.

"The frog joke," I said. "Lou has this great frog joke."

Glen smiled. "Frogs? Not chickens?"

"See? He wants to hear it. He'll love it."

Lou sighed. "Okay. But don't blame me. It wasn't my idea."

She wiped her hands on her napkin, propped her elbows
on the table, and rearranged her face. I thought of it as Lou
putting on her show face. She could animate her eyes—
make the shades of blue in them shift and dance—and raise

her chin to just the right height: I'm about to say something you'll want to hear. Trust me.

"So, there was this frog, with a really wide mouth—I mean wide—who lived in a barnyard…"

"They have chickens on this farm?" asked Glen.

"They have everything on this farm," I said. She went through the joke in all its excruciating detail. When at long last the frog came upon the snake, and Lou pursed her lips innocently—wide-mouth frog, what wide-mouth frog, no wide-mouth frogs around here—I giggled and raised a hand. She smacked it.

"You've still got it," I said. Our hands clasped across the table, we looked at the guys, who were looking from their plates to each other. They didn't get it. But so what? We would school them. We would bring them around.

Glen waved a tiny drumstick. "Did I mention there must be a dozen chickens, right here on my plate?"

Back at the apartment later that night, Lou was in the bathroom brushing her teeth. I took her by the elbow and pulled her back to our room. I pointed at the chalkboard. She looked up, white paste bubbling over her lips. She opened her mouth in surprise, and then blurted, "Ugh!" She had to lean forward to catch some spilling toothpaste spit in her hand.

The quote began, "So, these are the wings, eh?" Glen was on the board.

IT HAD BEEN FOUR MONTHS, AND THEY WERE AT A KIND of stalemate. They loved each other, they said. But Glen hated Toronto: he was homesick for mountains and rain and people who weren't in a hurry. When we spent time with Glen, I got the feeling he existed on a different channel: we were tuned to some heavy-duty crime show, *The*

National, the six-o'clock news; he, I don't know—*The Nature of Things*? It didn't help that he lived right across the street from Maple Leaf Gardens. He and his sister, a lawyer, had a place several floors up, and on nights the Leafs played in town, he could open the window and lean out over the drunken fans spilling out onto Carleton Street and watch this great boisterous wave of humanity pass below the window. I was envious. They felt surrounded.

So, Glen was thinking of going back to the West Coast. Lou was torn between being the supportive girlfriend—"I love you! Do what makes you happy!"—and wanting to handcuff him to a lamppost at Yonge and Dundas. Or hire a hypnotist to wipe Vancouver from his memory. We'd chosen "Should I Stay or Should I Go" by the Clash as his personal anthem, hoping to shame him into making a decision—the one she wanted him to make.

I liked Glen: his cheesy jokes that were so much like Lou's, his friendly manner, his odd hang-ups. He worried constantly about his hair, and once tried to give Lou the money to buy him a new hair dryer. He was too embarrassed to bring it to the counter himself. Louisa refused: *If you need it that much, you can at least own up to it.* She and I went on about how pathetic that was, but really, you couldn't be mad at Glen. He was kind-hearted, self-deprecating. He had a clever yet unassuming way of expressing himself. He'd written on the quote board, "I'm like a sponge: when I study, I soak everything up. The problem is I drip all the way to the test."

But I was fed up. If he really wanted to be with Lou, like he said, what was the problem? Or, if he had to go, he should gulp and get on a plane. The uncertainty was torture.

Our whole six-roommate unit was in a mid-year funk. We'd started the school year with designated shelf space in the fridge—drawing cartoons on our milk jugs with markers to identify them—but now we were turning our heads away when we opened the door to bravely thrust a hand into the midst of the cartons and wrappings, the overripe fruit and the mouldy cheese, the caked-over pots and rancid bacon and stray olives, hoping for the best. Also, once you were in our student co-op, you were in, no matter how many eons ago you'd written your last exam. We lived among an assortment of wan, undernourished characters who had, in some distant past, attended Ryerson. On bad days it felt like Hotel California. We shared closet space with cockroaches, and Casey once dramatically caught a mouse in a lampshade—too slippery for the rodent to scramble out of—carried it outside, and let it go. The fire alarm went off at least once a week, in the middle of the night, and Lou always wanted to heed it and I never did and we would battle it out till she would get up and drag me by an arm out of bed, out into the hallway, and down the stairwell with its landings sticky from beer spills.

Adding a layer of anxiety to our gloom was the looming war in the Gulf. I couldn't fathom why George Bush would want to go into Iraq. I felt there was a piece of critical information I was lacking. Maybe some last-ditch diplomacy would forestall an attack. This was a topic we journalism students talked about after class over pitchers of beer at the Library, the upstairs lounge at the Imperial Pub, a dingy Dundas Street bar. The Library was lined with bookshelves and crowded with pool tables, and its name was convenient for undergrad humour: "I'll see you after class at the *Library*," we loved to declare. Wink, wink. Lou and Glen seldom joined us. Glen's issue wasn't only Toronto. It was journalism itself. And Lou was doubting it too: that little molecule of uncertainty I'd seen emerge when Simon first told her RTA was way more fun had multiplied. And now it was spreading.

It had begun with our first reporting class, a day-long affair each week, for which we would be handed an assignment upon arriving at 9 a.m., having barely downed a coffee, and expected to submit an article, researched and containing quotes from real interview subjects, by four o'clock that afternoon. This, we were given to understand, was what daily life would be like for a reporter at a major daily newspaper.

Our assignments varied. We were sent to conduct man-on-the-street interviews about some issue that was "hot" in the news. We were sent to council meetings, the courthouse, inquest court. While trying not to get lost; while trying to find the right people to interview and then work up the courage to approach them (knowing that any question we could throw at them would be hopelessly naive); we were constantly aware that there were five *W*s we would have to be able to answer when we finally sat down to write—five *W*s, plus *How*. One mustn't forget *How*. And that wasn't all. You needed to understand the context, which might constitute ten years of *W*s and *How*s, and you had a day to learn that context and boil it down to a line or two. Plus, you had to find the newest thing, the significant change in this decade-old situation: it was your job to bring the news of this particular, press-stopping *Who*, *What*, *Where*, *When*, or *Why* to the masses.

Or, in our case, to the professor. My prof was an American draft dodger who slouched against the chalkboard while teaching us the principles of lateral thinking—the famous news piece on the spike in birth rates nine months after a New York City blackout being a prime example. His sweaters were constantly smeared with chalk dust. I would sit there asking myself: Where is the unexpected angle? The story no one will see unless I point it out? Black-clad professor. White dust. Vietnam. Basement classroom. Every week I came up empty.

It was all terrifying. I forced myself to gulp and get through, because I figured it was the only way I would learn how to write wondrous, exciting magazine articles that would change the way people saw the world—my big dream!

Louisa, though, began to flag early on. Problem number one, for her: the inverted pyramid. "It's oppressive," she said to me. She didn't want facts laid out in order of importance. She wanted drama. Charged moments, dialogue and tears. She'd been acting since the age of ten, when she took part in a production by Burlington Student Theatre and was told by its artistic director that she showed great promise. She'd spent what seemed like half of our final year of high school struggling with the role of Laura in Tennessee Williams's *The Glass Menagerie*—and had relished the struggle as only Lou could. The drama teacher that year had her students keep a journal. Lou's was filled with variations on the following: "She's so wishy-washy. I can't relate to her!" And: "It's hard to find what makes her tick. Playing the game, I got stuck frequently. WHAT IS LAURA!? Ugh!"

Apparently, she was having the same problem "clicking" with journalism, but without the excitement that came with being part of a stage production. I strove not to take this personally—not to feel abandoned. We'd never made a pact that we would follow the same path to the ends of the earth, had we?

I also tried to be a grown-up about my increasingly lonesome homework tea breaks.

One night, a few days before my nineteenth birthday, we were in our room together studying. Well, *I* was studying, on my bed with my back against the wall, my Canadian politics textbook open in my lap. Lou sat at her desk, yet again writing furiously in her journal.

She was obviously working something out. I left the room to go put on the kettle. I could still make tea: tea did not require her participation. Lou had always had her own room, while I'd shared mine with Wendy. Maybe she just needed space. The fact was, I was spending more and more nights in the room next door, with Simon. You might think this would have solved the space issue. But who wants to be alone in bed on one side of a wall while her best friend is in bed on the other with some guy? There was never a confrontation between us over this. She never said to me, "You couldn't pick a guy on another floor, at least?" She never suggested that I had turned my living arrangement with her into a living arrangement with him, though I wonder if that's how she felt. She had her own guy just a few blocks away, yes. But Glen lived with his sister; Lou lived with me. They didn't exactly have a private haven in either place.

In the morning I was catching a GO train to Burlington to visit my parents, to celebrate my birthday, so she'd have a couple of nights to herself, anyway. Or she and Glen would have a couple of nights to *them*selves. Either way, maybe my absence would help.

THE NEXT MORNING, I OPENED MY EYES AND CRANED MY neck and looked at the clock: 8:45. I had to catch my train in an hour. The unit was still quiet. I dressed quickly and leaned into the window ledge to peer outside. The city was coated in a layer of frost: it had gone from concrete to crystal overnight. I felt the cold creeping in through the cracks around the frame. I turned to Louisa, her comforter pulled up to her chin. She blinked.

"It's cold out."

"Mmm," she said, still sleepy. "Take the PATH."

"No kidding." You could walk underground almost all the way from Ryerson to Union Station.

"Say hi to Phyllis and Sandy." We liked to call my parents by their first names.

"I will."

"Have fun."

"I'll try."

Our eyes met, and Lou smiled, understanding the mixed bag of emotions that came with going home. Everything about our exchange seemed normal. Except that I could feel her waiting for me to leave.

TWO DAYS LATER I RAN INTO LOUISA AT THE CORNER NEAR Lake Devo. I'd just walked up from the train. We fell into step, cutting through the quad and crossing the intersection near our building.

"How was your trip?"

"Okay. Matthew gave me a bear for my birthday."

"Cute."

"And Dad called me a slut."

"What?"

"I don't know. It had to do with Simon. I said I wasn't going to marry him and he freaked."

"Oh my god. Marry him?"

"That's what I thought. But I guess, to him…"

"Maybe."

We'd been eating a seafood feast, in my honour. Salmon, scallops, crab. Mom reported that a cousin was about to embark on her third marriage, and I said, "You're kidding? How many times can one person get married?"

Wendy had jumped in, eyes a-sparkle. "Wait till you and Simon get married!" I set her straight—"We're not, he's just my boyfriend"—and that's when Dad let me have it. Mom shouted at him across the table. "Don't talk to your daughter like that!"

A piece of crab leg dangled from his fork, white and stringy. "Well, I want to know. What are her plans?"

"I have no plans," I'd said quietly.

Lou and I crossed the street and turned down our block. "Anyway, how are *you*?"

"I'd like to drop-kick Glen into the lake."

"Lou, violence isn't the answer."

"What if I cut his hair while he's sleeping?"

"You could hide his hair dryer."

We'd crossed the street and were passing by the youth hostel on our block.

"I could dangle it out the window and threaten to drop it till he makes up his mind."

We laughed. A woman stepped in front of us, forcing us to stop. She'd been hanging back by a staircase, smoking, a figure I'd only half registered out of the corner of my eye. She pointed her cigarette at Lou.

"I wouldn't laugh, honey. My pimp's looking for a redhead."

Her makeup was thick—globby mascara, wide swaths of eyeliner—so it was tough to guess how old she was. Fine lines about the mouth. Leather miniskirt. Fishnets. This was January.

We stepped around her, I to her right, Lou to her left, in our preppy wool jackets. "What's the matter?" the woman said, sneering. We passed stiffly. She called after us, raising her voice, "Don't worry! I'll let him know you're interested."

We kept walking. We didn't look back.

SIX

Typo

LIVING AWAY FROM HOME, LOUISA AND I HAD QUICKLY become proud of our frugality. Cutting corners, like buying generic brands at the grocery store, was satisfying. But we hadn't gotten too far into the school year before we'd become unnerved, almost alarmed, at seeing our bank balances drop. It wasn't that we'd miscalculated. We knew we could each survive the year on our savings—but only *just*. The prospect of a whole school year without being able to cover too many fun nights out, or some unforeseen expense, loomed. It was overwhelming. It was depressing.

The solution was obvious. We needed jobs. The question was where to find these jobs. In a restaurant, maybe? But neither of us relished the thought of late shifts or the walk home alone through downtown streets at one in the morning.

I'd begun haunting a bookshop in the mini mall across the street from the Eaton Centre. It was one in a little chain with the best-stocked newsstand and magazine racks in the city. One day I told Louisa that this store, called Lichtman's, was the place I really wished I could work, but I figured it would be impossible.

"Why do you say that?"

I shrugged. "What do I know about working in a bookstore?"

"They'd train you."

I shook my head. "It'd be too good to be true."

"After you get your English and politics essays done this weekend," she said, "you're going straight there to apply for a job." It was rare for Lou to take her bossy tone with me. Her nostrils flared. I would swear her freckles deepened in colour, too.

"Fine. I'll do it."

I did better. After class that day I walked to the mall and into the store and, before I could talk myself out of it, I nervously asked for an application. Lucky me, the manager had just lost a couple of part-timers. She decided—likely inspired by her own desperation—that I looked reliable. She asked when I could start.

"Monday," I told her. "I'd like to finish a couple of papers first."

"You'll have more papers to write. And exams. Do you think you can handle this?"

"Definitely. I worked part-time in high school, too. I just need to rethink my schedule."

She nodded sagely. "You're thinking about time management. Good for you. You'll do just fine."

I booked my first training shift for Monday at five. Lichtman's was open till ten or eleven every night, and though I hadn't wanted to do so from a restaurant, I found I had no qualms about walking home alone late from the bookstore. Obviously, I was willing to compromise for a job I actually wanted.

Lou, meanwhile, through a chance meeting with its manager, was offered a job at the fur salon at the Bay. I thought she'd turn it down: these were heady times for anti-fur activism. But she jumped at the chance and began work immediately. So that quickly, our money problems were solved: the universe had provided. I worked in the building directly to the north of the Eaton Centre, and Lou in the one directly to the south. We'd sometimes find ourselves working parallel shifts, her selling furs, and me books and magazines, with that massive mall we were coming to know so well hulking between us.

ONE AFTERNOON, WE SAT TOGETHER ON A CONCRETE bench embedded with chipped stone, facing the central fountain in the Eaton Centre, each eating a raspberry Yogen Früz, the red swirls rising out of the paper cups in our hands like massive dollops of icing. Lou was on a break. She'd asked me to come by on my way to the night shift at the bookstore.

The mall was abuzz. Groups of students like clouds of gnats blew past. A tour group stood nearby, their cameras pointed at the fountain. They were waiting for the spout of water in the middle to shoot up a full storey—as it was programmed to do every ten minutes. I had just dug into my cup with the tiny purple spoon for a fresh mouthful of yogurt when I noticed Louisa blinking furiously.

"Holy shit, you're crying."

"Sorry."

"Are you okay? What is it?" I braced myself, expecting more from the Glen saga. The fountain shot up, eliciting gasps and murmurs. A light spray fell on our cheeks. Barely audible, she told me. Her breast was infected. Or she had breast cancer. Something. Something horrible. The nipple was red, and cracked, and leaking. "It's gross. Later, I'll—could you—look at it?"

"Yes. Of course. In the meantime, try not to worry." Wrong thing to say. She opened her mouth but I spoke first. "You don't know that it's anything. Really."

"It's sore. It hurts."

"It could be totally unrelated to anything."

"Yeah. I know."

For months, I'd hardly thought of the lump that the surgeon had cut from under her left arm, the one she'd been told had contained those two "iffy" cells. It had been nearly a year since she'd spent those few days in hospital. She was saying nothing now about a lump. And yet.

When I saw it, I could say she was crazy instead of sick. A big fat worrier. I was the rational one, after all. But I only wanted to *say* it was nothing—and there was nothing rational in that.

AS WE WALKED BACK TO LOUISA'S JOB AT THE FUR SALON, I felt her pressing her distress below the surface. This was okay. Leaving her with her boss, Hugo, was almost as good as leaving her with her mom or dad. Hugo was a warm, generous, compassionate boss who took an interest in his employees' well-being. He'd become a kind of surrogate uncle figure in her life.

All the same, I felt weird about the fur salon. It wasn't so acceptable anymore to go around wearing a mink coat, or to kill an animal just for its silky pelt. I asked Lou if this bothered her, and she shrugged. She was not susceptible to social justice "causes" in the way that seemed almost a requirement of others in our circumstance: that is, being students, being young. From her perspective, she'd been offered a job by a person with a good heart, in a place that would give her the chance to help people feel good about themselves—and warm. Also, I suspect it felt a touch glamorous.

Inside the glass walls, I let her put me in a three-quarter-length, green, brushed-leather jacket and spin me in the mirror. "It looks gorgeous on you."

I rolled my eyes.

"You underestimate your looks all the time."

"That's better than overestimating, isn't it?"

"I think people see you how you see yourself."

"So, I could make myself better-looking just by thinking I am?" She nodded. "But I don't want to think about my looks at all."

"That's part of your problem."

"You *know* why I gave up my dream of becoming a lawyer."

She sighed. "I know. Your mother told you you'd have to dress up for court."

"My mother knows me very well."

"There's nothing wrong with looking nice."

This was an old disagreement between us, strangely comforting, but I had to go. I exchanged a look with her that meant *We'll talk later*. She nodded.

I quickly made my way back through the mall. I would just make it to Lichtman's on time. I was quietly proud of working there. We sold *Harper's* and *Hello!* and *Der Spiegel* and the *China Morning News*—newspapers in Arabic, French, and Italian, and every obscure periodical in the country, from *Opera Canada* and *CineAction* to *Canadian Stamp News* and the *Canadian Horse Journal*. Our regulars included several of my Ryerson profs; Bill, who smelled of doorways and subway entranceways, and would come in asking if we had anything for, say, "twenty-eight cents" while offering a sticky butterscotch candy from his coat pocket; and famous authors such a Peter C. Newman, a tall grim man in a tall dark hat.

On Sunday mornings a gaggle of men would be outside waiting for the doors to open so they'd have first crack at our limited stock of the Sunday *New York Times*. We carried both versions, the thinner national and the bulkier metro, and for most of these guys, if the one they wanted was gone, the other wouldn't do. Before working here, I'd had no idea that such people existed, for whom a newspaper mattered that much. I didn't know there were devoted readers of everything from *Jane's Defence* to *Quill & Quire*. I couldn't believe I was paid to hang out here. When the store was quiet, I would tidy the magazine racks, which meant shoving a hand into the narrow, tiered slots to fish out the wayward subscription cards crumpled at the bottom. I went home at night bearing paper cuts, scraped knuckles, and staple wounds, and sheathed in a layer of dust, feeling that I was earning my keep.

Meg, the manager who'd hired me, was an English scholar on the side—or more like she was an English scholar managing a bookshop on the side. In a different way, she'd become for me what Hugo was for Lou: an older, wiser person with, it seemed, my best interests at heart. She had short-cropped hair, wore Doc Martin boots, and lusted after Jean-Luc Picard, a magazine cut-out of whom she kept above her desk in the store's cubbyhole office. After closing, when you were hunched there counting your cash, hoping you wouldn't be short, Picard would look down on you with his shiny Star Trek head and his half-smile, seeming to know exactly how things would go.

That night, a woman with long curly hair and an air of agitation marched into the store and asked if we sold the *Canadian Theatre Review*. I led the way, pleased that I remembered shuffling it around on a recent straightening binge. I was still learning our extensive stock, and even a week before, I might have been stumped. But instead of buying one, she took every copy out of the rack, crouched on the floor with them, and pulled a pencil out of her coat. I was alarmed. "What are you doing?"

She looked up at me with some annoyance. "I'm fixing a typo."

"You're what?"

She'd contributed an article and claimed that a wrong word in a sentence had altered the meaning of an entire paragraph. She showed me the page. "Look. It says the opposite of what it was meant to say." She was going to newsstands all around the city, trying to fix as many as she could. I returned to my post at the cash and left her to it.

Back at our place that night, I described the scene to Lou.

"You let her carry on?"

"She was only crossing out a word. I mean, she was right. It was like, 'can' instead of 'can't'. Like one letter changed everything. The sentence made perfect sense. There's no way you'd know there was a typo."

"So, she's going around fixing every copy with a pencil? I mean, how many copies would there be?"

"Well, it's not like the *Globe and Mail*. You can probably only get them at a handful of bookstores."

"What about subscribers?"

"Yeah, good point. Maybe she'll get their addresses and go knocking on their doors."

"Pardon me, sorry to trouble you, but could I just have a look at that magazine on your coffee table? There's a mistake in one of my articles."

"I'll just fix it up with this pencil…Oh my. You read *Border Crossings* too? We must be soul mates!"

We laughed. We were sitting in the common room with mugs of hot tea, rare for us these days.

"What did she look like?"

"I don't know. Pinched. You'll tell me, right, if I ever get that intense? I mean it."

"How could I not? You'd be insufferable." She blew on her tea, making a little wave in the cup. "And you'll tell me?"

"Um. You are that intense."

"Hey!"

"It's part of your charm."

We sipped our tea. A silence settled between us. Our earlier conversation by the fountain in the mall, and Lou's sense of panic, thoughts of which I'd succeeded in setting aside all evening, seemed to push rudely right up into the quiet. I stood up and placed my mug on the counter. "How about—do you want to show me now?"

Fear flickered in her eyes. "Okay."

We walked down the hall to our room. We shut the door. She peeled off her shirt and snapped open her bra. The nipple looked raw and sore. As far as I understood, breast cancer had to do with lumps, not cracked nipples. But what was this? What could it be? I looked at Lou helplessly.

She went to see the doctor at the Ryerson clinic—the same guy who'd put us on the pill. He took her off it.

"Why?"

"I don't know. Something about the hormones."

The doctor also put her on an antibiotic, and she soon healed. Despite an ultrasound, blood tests, and other investigations, he couldn't name what had afflicted her. It was just some freak infection that, thankfully, went away. But I was spooked. The business with Iraq had sort of died down. I began to care less about war and politics, less about the American president and the beleaguered people of a distant country, and more about what was going to happen to Louisa, and to me.

The facts were all there in my mind: I dug up the files, reviewed the transcripts. I kept landing on "two iffy cells." This was all Louisa had told me about the pathology results on the lump under her arm. I'd been relieved. Now I thought of the woman in the store, so desperate to obliterate that typo. She could cross it out all she liked, but the mistake was printed; it existed. It was too late to reverse it completely. Those "two iffy cells" had transferred from Louisa's arm to my mind. They wouldn't go away.

SEVEN

Undertow

MOM WALKED INTO THE KITCHEN WHILE I WAS POURING water in the coffee maker. It was Sunday morning and I'd come home for the weekend. "Hi," I said. "How are you?"

"How do you think?" Sharp words, a clunk. I turned to see my journal where she'd smacked it down on the table. She was wearing an old blue bathrobe, and her brown eyes had darkened to a thick mud.

"Oh, I must have left that downstairs. Thanks."

"What is *wrong* with you? What's *happened* to you? Your brother—"

The glass coffee pot was in my hand, tilted above the machine, all the water poured out. "My brother? Which one? What about him?"

She stabbed her long, knobby index finger into the journal's cover. "How could you leave that lying around where Matthew might find it?"

I slid the pot into place and pressed On. A red light flashed, followed by a hiss. "Why are you so upset?" The question dissolved into the charged force field surrounding her. "Wait a minute. You read it?"

"You leave something lying around my house, I'll read it if I damn well please."

Woah. *You don't live here anymore*, she was saying. *You're not a part of this household*. "Oh. Okay. But if it upset you to read it, maybe next time—"

"How could you write something like that? What's wrong with you?" Her voice rose; the words lost shape and form. She was starting to cry.

The first pages of the journal were filled with a bill bissett poem I'd copied from my first-year Can-lit textbook, *The New Oxford Book of Canadian Verse in English*, edited by Margaret Atwood. Titled "christ I wouldnt know normal if I saw it when," the poem was three pages of unpunctuated, tantalizingly disturbing questions made up of words spelled in bissett's idiosyncratic way. For example, *you* is *yu*; *thought* becomes *thot*; and *some* appears as *sum*. We weren't studying this particular poem, but I'd read it one evening and copied it out. I was fascinated by how it contained no commas or periods but still made sense. I was also intrigued by the effect of those oddly spelled words. *Sum* was still *some*. The original meaning held. But if a word could be said to pulse with its own faint glow, the light coming off this one had changed. What emanated from *sum* was slightly sinister. I wanted to understand why.

Mom's reaction, though, had nothing to do with this. The poem was political and crude, borderline X-rated. That's why she was upset.

I pressed my fingers into the back of my neck. I spoke carefully. "Mom, I didn't write that poem. I just copied it out of a textbook."

"A textbook? That's what they're teaching you at that so-called university?"

The coffee machine began to gurgle and drip. Mom pulled at the blue fleece belt around her waist, tightening the knot. She'd clearly been awake all night, her sense of betrayal building: Who was I, this person who professed to be her daughter and had gone off to university? There was no way to explain the appeal of the poem. I didn't get why bissett only sometimes spelled phonetically, or how a different vowel here or there could change a word's personality—but it did, and that made me curious. I was also caught by the wildly ranting poem as a whole, which was smushed together from the same mulch of fear, optimism, and confusion that I carried around with me everywhere. It condemned yet forgave, an enormous blurt that finally added up to empathy: This is what we are. We're messy. We can't always trust ourselves. Let's admit that much.

But Mom was caught somewhere between words like *screw* and *cum*. I wasn't going to be able to fix this. I fumbled for words. "Um. Can I have it back?"

"Take it." She pushed it toward me across the table.

AFTER THE BILL BISSETT INCIDENT, LOUISA TOLD ME THAT Mom was right: I should have been more careful. Once she'd written an angry "letter" in her journal to her mom, to later find it torn out, and a pointed response in its place. The journal Lou kept our first year away from home was not so provocative—and not as different from her earlier volumes as mine was.

Our respective writing habits had first flourished in high school. Journal entries, poems, a blurring of the two. We composed on the Ikea mattress opened onto the floor from the pullout couch in Louisa's room. On the tufted white carpeting on the floor of my bedroom. Or we wrote alone and read to each other over the phone, or traded compositions by our lockers in the morning. My poems often rhymed, followed an iambic beat, and were divided into tidy stanzas. Lou's contained short broken lines running down the page—they were crafty and quick.

Lou insisted I was the better writer. But I didn't like how my poems went on and on. I wished I could make them like hers: short and casual and sometimes funny. I began using up all my three-ring binder paper for compositions and scribbling my class notes on the backs of rough drafts. Soon I was presenting new poems to Lou several times a week. She bragged and showed my work around—especially the pieces concerning her own thwarted love life—and requests began to come in. For a time, I found myself called on to pen poems for heartbroken classmates. "What happened?" I'd ask, my notebook open. "Tell me the whole story." I'd write furiously while they poured out their sorrow, and later that night, in my bedroom, I'd scribble lines and cross them out, struggling to make their pain and misfortune rhyme.

I retain no specimens from this unexpected occupation; I gave them all to their subjects. I've no doubt they were devoid of subtlety, never mind humour. Nonetheless, I was awed by the gratitude my efforts inspired. It's a powerful thing to have your heartache packed into verse: the words on the page, the hard shape of it, the hint of music rising from even the clunky work of an amateur. I like to think that, by acknowledging it, by attempting to capture and express it, each of those poetic gestures lent legitimacy to a private anguish.

Louisa once wrote such a poem for me, composed of soothing, rhyming couplets: "I know it's hard to hide / all the hurt you feel inside," and "I know it's hard to pretend / that your broken heart will mend." When she handed me the finished product she laughed and said, "Sorry. I gave up." She'd had trouble finding a suitable closing rhyme. I must still have the poem somewhere, perhaps in the old blue luggage case where I keep some things from those years, but I don't need to hunt it down. I still remember the lines by heart:

> I promise a day will come when you'll see
> that what is to be will be—
>
> when you'll be over him
> and off on another whim.

Stupid word, *whim*. But the thing is, it worked. I felt better. How silly, to be falling apart over this guy. That was maybe the difference between Louisa and me—she knew when to let something go, when something wasn't worth agonizing over. At least, in a poem. Me, I latched onto poem-making like a toddler with a fierce grip on a toy. I wrestled with the words; I squeezed them for all they were worth. I forgot all about life before this discovery, this purpose.

Now I was writing more poems than ever, and, like bissett's, they were not sentimental pastoral pieces. One, my reaction to a guest lecture on the glass ceiling still in place for women in journalism, was a tirade against all the ways I considered women held themselves back. It starts like this: "Ladies. Puhleeze. / Wake up and / smell / the perfume / in the boardroom / no-one's forcing you to vacuum / It's your choice, Joyce." Yeesh.

Louisa's voice never altered. Its intensity ebbed and flowed, but no edge had crept in, no arrogance. She wrote in a tall, blue hardcover notebook with 8.5 by 11 pages. It had been a Christmas present from her mother. She hadn't come near to filling it the previous year. Most of the entries she wrote now were about her new obsession: Glen. About the sudden onset of her feelings for him and how over-whelming they were. About her unsettling attraction to him—Lou, who considered herself a "true" Virgo, did not like to feel like she wasn't in control. Glen made her feel that way.

I think sometimes of the avid correspondences histori-cally kept up between writers, and by writers and their closest friends, and I wonder whether Lou and I wouldn't both, in other circumstances, have been destined for a literary life. The journals and poems gave us a way of communicating with each other that we couldn't always accomplish out loud. In conversation, without that pause in which you can chew on the pen lid and ponder, without that interlude of solitude, it's so hard to figure out how to say what you mean. I always felt a thrill and a pride—*I am her chosen one*—when Louisa set her journal before me, open to a recent page. I read eagerly: an eagerness tinged with fear and excitement. What would her fat, left-leaning scrawl reveal this time? What surprise, what new problem, was in store?

WE MOVED BACK TO BURLINGTON IN MAY, LADEN WITH boxes. We settled in our old bedrooms, returned to our old jobs as camp counsellors. Though we enjoyed the world of camp as much as ever, each day felt like a holding pattern, an interruption in what was now our real life, away from home.

For Lou, the first month of summer was a period of intense waiting: Glen had decided that, if he succeeded in his appli-cation to the broadcast stream at Ryerson, which had limited enrolment and was highly competitive, he would return to

Toronto in the fall and finish his degree. If not, he'd stay in Vancouver and go to the University of British Columbia.

On June 16 Glen got his letter. I have a copy of Lou's journal from back then. The entry for that day reads, in part:

> I guess this is the way it's supposed to be…Glen isn't coming back.
>
> I have to stare at that for a while. I can't believe it's true. He's staying in B.C. forever because that's his home and where he belongs. I have taken all his pictures off my board, out of my frame. His calendar off the wall. His gifts off the shelf. The writing pad with all my letters to him out of my drawer like he never existed. I don't know how to deal with this. I am in shock. I keep crying and then being very calm. He was not meant to be the love of my life. I will not marry him. I am in shock. I have to call A—.

A week later she wrote that they had decided to remain friends because they meant too much to each other not to be. (But also, that he was being a wimp and a coward.) Two weeks after that she met a guy named Zach, planned to go to the movies with him, and was stood up. She made a brave phone call demanding an explanation and was told he was worried about their age difference—he was twenty-four, she nineteen. We ran into him that week at the Pig & Whistle, the bar by the lake we hung out in that summer.

"A— had a fight with him about it," she wrote. "She told him he was being stupid and all the things A— says to you when she thinks you're being a moron." After which he spoke to her again. Her record of the moment: "'I'm sorry,' he said. 'I didn't just ask you out because it was something to do. I like you but I'm on a teeter-totter here.' As he was telling me all this, I was staring into his awesome blue eyes and thinking that I just wanted to attack him." In that same entry, though, she labelled the Zach thing "lust" and the Glen thing "love." "That looks so stupid but it's true."

She was in mourning. She wrote a four-page poem in quatrains—to me, an alarming level of formality for her to adopt. She wrote to herself: "He made a decision. He had the balls to make a very difficult decision. But I do think he made the right one." Then all at once everything changed: she wasn't in mourning after all. She wasn't giving up. "He's in me—in my heart permanently," she wrote. But that was a mistake too, because ten days later, she fiercely declared in writing, "The truth is we're not right for each other. That's been the hardest to admit." It wasn't unusual for Louisa to rethink her feelings about a guy, but her flip-flops regarding Glen became so frequent and extreme I found it difficult to keep up. By the end of the summer she was convinced—maybe this time for good? I had no idea, really—that they couldn't be just friends. "It's really amazing what I can talk myself into," she wrote. "I love Glen—so much that it really scares me." She was often up till 2 a.m. for his Pacific Standard Time phone calls. These were the days before long-distance plans, and it was much cheaper to call after 11 p.m. Still, the bill arriving each month was like Judgment Day.

And I would say, when the subject arose, *Are you sure? Him? Really?*

Though Simon and I summered in the same city, we saw each other less and less as the weeks passed. In late August, I travelled with my family for a week's vacation in Myrtle Beach. The day we arrived, there was a commotion on the beach: a man had drowned in the undertow. People stood in groups on the beach, colourful and still: their bathing suits dripping, brown skin shimmering, bare feet half submerged in the fine sand. Their eyes were all turned toward the deceptively gentle surf, as if they were waiting for the man to reappear. His limp, wet body had been carried off on a stretcher, but it was the lapping salt water to which everyone looked. What had it done with him? Where had he gone?

The rest of our trip passed without major incident. Wendy and I spent our time in the warm water, or walking down the long, soft shore, barefoot and relaxed. We each met a boy. Or should I say "man"? Mine was a young firefighter from New York State, with whom I flirted more extensively than a person with a boyfriend back home should have. But I found it difficult to square the two worlds, and understood at once how betrayal happens, why lovers worry so obsessively while apart. I returned to Canada resolved to end my year-long relationship, which suddenly seemed frivolous, and prepared to work hard, and study well, and read insatiably—and to write as if my life depended on it. I promised myself to better learn my craft.

Back home, I dropped my suitcase on the floor of the bedroom I was again sharing with my sister—in some ways it was as if I'd never left—and went down to the kitchen to call Lou. I had to tell her about my new conviction. And ask her how I was going to break up with Simon. (And maybe share a few details about the firefighter.)

"Can you come over?" she said.

"When?"

"Now?"

I borrowed the car and drove across town.

When Lou opened the door, she opened her mouth, but nothing came out. I stood blinking in the doorway. I forgot all the things I'd planned to tell her, and thought instead of the man who'd drowned, the undertow grabbing his feet, tying knots around his legs. Maybe I could sweep in and wash that look out of Lou's eyes, draw it toward me across the threshold and recede.

IT WAS NESTLED IN HER UPPER LEFT ARM, MERE INCHES away from the one that had been removed about sixteen months before. We celebrated her twentieth birthday, August 27, 1991, in the Toronto General Hospital. The lump had been cut away by a surgeon, a neat incision left in its place: her third scar. A bunch of old friends drove in from Burlington. We took over one of the colourless lounges, and Lou's dad, who'd carted in a cooler of pop, ordered pizza. We should have been in a bar; we should have been dancing.

Lou, who looked no more diseased than the rest of us, made us laugh about the foul-smelling patient with whom she was sharing a room—some unpleasant gastrointestinal problem—though neither her plight, nor her roommate's, was really very funny.

We endured another period of waiting. We moved back into student housing, into a smaller unit on the fifteenth floor. Things seemed promising at first. Lou and I had splurged on our own rooms, but we'd chosen two that were side by side. Our old roommate Casey joined us in the new place. Like him, Lou was in Radio and Television Arts now. In one of her first assignments she wrote a personality profile of herself that described her mistaken detour into journalism: "She realized that along her misguided route, she had lost one very important thing. Well, it's bold, it's bursting and it's back. It's her zest for life, and it's back in high doses."

But there were shadows. We awaited results from the pathology tests. And there was Glen. Rather, there wasn't Glen. Louisa couldn't, or wouldn't, let him go. Every day, it seemed, was an about-face from the hope that they could make it work to the certainty that it was over. In the past I would have bit my tongue; but now, we began to argue. Glen's sister still lived in town, and against my advice—my pleading—Lou saw her frequently. One night, Glen's parents were in town, and Lou went out with them all for dinner, and came back telling me how she felt like part of the family. She called Glen, and by the end of the call he was planning a Christmas visit. Three months without that to look forward to and Lou might've actually moved on. But now...

My perspective was perhaps tinted by my own circumstances, involving young men who were actually in the vicinity. I broke up with Simon right after the school year started. Soon after, I told Louisa that there might be something in the offing with our friend Ryan. "I'll wait as long as it takes," he'd said to me one night at the bar, a startling confession made with such gentleness and near-absence of hope that I was won. Lou couldn't believe it. "Ryan? You can't go out with Ryan!"

I was stunned. "Why not? I like him."

"But he was *my* friend."

"What?"

"Ryan and Lee. I met them last year. They were my friends."

I was just inside the doorway to my room. She was in the hallway, looking in. She stood with her mouth slightly open, her lips moving, seeming to rework the words, to convince herself she'd said them. Finally, I spoke. "Are you interested in Ryan?"

She shook her head adamantly. "No."

"So, what's the problem?"

"I'm sorry. That's not what I meant. It's just. You don't match."

I retreated into my room. She turned and was gone. I listened to her walk to her room and sit down on the bed.

What was going on? I had been surprised at Ryan's interest; I'd always felt he harboured a crush on Lou. Had he given up on her, I wondered? Was I simply a consolation? And had she been enjoying that he was, in a sense, hers, even though she didn't want him? I had never thought we were the kind of friends who disagreed over their boyfriends and disapproved of each other's choices. But here we were, me against Glen and her against Ryan.

Some days later we fell into a discussion in the kitchen that seemed, at first, like safer ground. We were talking about Wendy, who was four years younger than me, and Lou's brother Miles, who was three years younger than her. Indeed, it was the two of them, out of all of our respective family members, whom we most often discussed, in part because we harboured a dream that they would someday fall in love, though their one-time "romance"—when Wendy was eleven and Miles twelve—had been short-lived and uneventful.

Maturity was the issue on the table. I no longer remember why, but I was trying to convince Lou that Miles was more grown-up than my sister. To make my point I brought up some serious trouble Miles had gotten into when he was younger. I was trying to show that he, literally, had more life experience under his belt, real life. We both knew he'd come out of the situation repentant, determined, changed. But Lou shouted at me from where she stood, on the other side of the island counter, above which hung the kitchen cupboards. She actually shouted, "So what are you saying? Wendy's better than him?"

"God no! I'm just trying to say he's been through more."

But the whole substance of our original discussion had dissolved. Now we were talking over each other, the volume rising, and it wasn't about who was more mature, but who was more "good," and, so far as Lou could tell, I had claimed Wendy as winner. It was absurd and frustrating. After I'd explained myself a dozen times or more, Lou sighed and gave in and said, "Okay, I see what you mean." But this was a lie. She neither believed me nor forgave me; she was merely tired. I had dug into a half-healed wound, and it didn't matter that I hadn't meant to do it.

During the situation with Miles, which had dragged on for months, I knew Lou had been troubled, worried. But I'd had no idea how deep her distress had gone. And though I knew she'd been like a second mother to her brothers, her protectiveness, as fierce and pure as that of a bear for its cub, startled me.

I should have remembered this later, how easy it was to miss what was really going on with her, especially during a crisis. The fight was sudden and violent and it hurt, but it didn't last, and we soon behaved as though it hadn't happened.

LOUISA STOOD IN THE MIDDLE OF HER BEDROOM, WEARING her floppy pink track pants and a beige camisole, reaching her right hand straight up toward the ceiling. I knelt beside her on the bed, pressing my fingers into the pocket beneath her arm. There was definitely something there. It wasn't muscle. It wasn't cartilage. Not bone. It was tiny but hard, and unmistakably rooted beneath her skin. This time, it wasn't the only one. There was another in her groin.

We were only a few weeks into the fall term, progressively being nudged by our professors into ever-more-demanding— and exciting—journalistic roles. That afternoon I'd constructed my first newscast. I'd conducted interviews. I'd "summed up." I'd stood with my hand around the microphone, my chin in the air, and signed off. *This is Anita Lahey, at Victoria and Dundas in Toronto, for RCTV News.*

When I got home, I found Lou sitting straight up on the edge of her bed.

She'd smiled. I thought she might be on the verge of saying something about Glen—their relationship continued, of course, with all its long-distance difficulty. They were remarkably stubborn. Or just stuck. But maybe this was one of their good days. I, meanwhile, had begun seeing Ryan, and Lou had seemed to let go of her objections, or she was at least keeping them to herself. When she'd told Glen about us, he'd blurted out, "That's great! They'll be so good together." Looking a bit sheepish, she'd reported this to me after one of their epic phone calls. I silently thanked him.

But she didn't have either of our boyfriends on her mind today. Instead, she began to tell me about her doctor's appointment that morning. She'd sat between her parents, facing the doctor, her father on her right and her mother on her left. The doctor's hands were folded on the desk. "I stared at them the whole time. After we sat down there was this silence. His eyes shifted. Then the silence broke. He sighed. This long, long sigh." He spoke of Lou's recurrent unusual skin growths. He was concerned enough to recommend treatment "as soon as possible."

Lou's parents posed a stream of questions. Hospitals. Specialists. Procedures. Treatments. Lou sat with her hands on the arms of the chair, staring at the doctor's hands. If she didn't move, if she stayed very still and never moved—if the doctor's hands never moved—

She got up. She had to go to the bathroom. She walked into a stall, closed the latch, and then slammed her hand against the door until her hand hurt so much that she started to cry. When the hot tears stopped, she left the stall, splashed cold water on her face at the sink, and walked back to the room that now seemed crowded, way too crowded.

On the way home, she asked her mother if she really had it. The C-word. Not the word she and I had decided as fourteen-year-olds was the most vile piece of language on the planet, but this new word, equally ugly, worse. Her mother turned to her and said, "Yes."

Malignant melanoma, he'd called it.

"We have to take them out," she told me now, as I pulled my finger away from the lump. She sounded as though she and Dr. Q, her new oncologist, were old hands at this, partners in crime. "I'm going to see the surgeon tomorrow."

"Aren't they doing anything else?" They. It was always "they." How long could they keep cutting her open and taking lumps out? What if they couldn't keep up?

She'd been told that after the surgery she would start on a drug called levamisole, an immune booster. "It's a kind of immunotherapy."

Immunotherapy. I clung to this development fiercely, because there was another C-word I did not wish to hear. As long as that word wasn't mentioned, the other seemed less important. What was cancer without chemotherapy? Without hair loss and puke? Not *real* cancer, surely. "He says my immune system isn't fighting hard enough, and if we can get it working right, I shouldn't get any more lumps."

I was resorting to "they," but she had picked up this "we" business. *We* were also going for more tests, ultrasounds, a CAT-scan, to suss out any more—tumours. That's what they were. Time to move on from "lump." Face facts. But I tried not to listen when she told me the survival rate. We were both sitting on the bed now. I watched her fingers with the chewed nails *tap tap tap* on her knee. How could I not hear it? Fifty percent. Fifty-fifty.

We could flip a coin on her life.

EIGHT

Late-Night Snack

FOR A TIME, LOUISA'S DIAGNOSIS CHANGED LITTLE IN OUR daily lives. That was how I chose to view the situation. It may have been how she allowed me, or even wanted me, to see it. If your closest friend behaves as though it's perfectly normal to be in and out of hospital, taking drugs you can barely pronounce, routinely measuring tumours as though she could manage this like anything else, from groceries to exams to fights with her boyfriend, well…who was I to suggest she couldn't?

It was November, colourless and cool. Lou was back in hospital for the second time since she'd been tagged with the C-word. The first had been for a planned operation to remove lumps in her arm and leg. The surgeon had decided it would be prudent to cut away not just the tumour from her leg but also the surrounding lymph nodes. He performed a groin dissection, leaving her with a twenty-centimetre incision crossing her bikini line and curving down her leg. She spent two days dizzy and puking from the anesthetic. Nonetheless, she returned to our apartment lump-free once more and wrote in her journal: *I am so happy now with* RTA *and I want to get involved in the Theatre Association and Glen is coming on Dec. 26. I love my life! I haven't been this happy with where my life was going in such a long time. I'm going to be fine—I have to believe that.*

She also got defiant. *Dear my Cancer*, she wrote. *You are not going to get me!! I'm sorry; I know you are trying to put a damper on my wonderful life, but it's not going to work. You might as well quit now.*

Three days later, her leg puffed up. Infection. She'd barely unpacked from her last trip to the hospital. *Here I am*, she wrote next, *back in the hospital with a swollen thigh. Same wing, same room, same bed at Toronto General.*

I was her loyal delivery person: I brought in a steady stream of cards and gifts from friends. Nothing from me. I figured I should change that. I brought her recorder to class. I would fill a tape with well-wishes. An audio get-well card. The idea was inspired. Lee was "in her corner"; Ryan's expectations were high; Sunita and Rose sent their love. Spence sang, off-key: *Show 'em you're a tiger—Lou! Show 'em what you can do!* Our friends teased and cajoled her. They said this "cancer thing" was nothing she couldn't handle. They cheered her on like a ballplayer approaching the plate.

I met Ryan and Lee in the Junkyard—a downstairs café the day never saw. We preferred it to the massive cafeteria in Jorgenson Hall. We sat in one of the deep booths eating chicken fingers and fries. When I played them the tape, I had one of those flashes you get sometimes, where you see the moment you're in as a scene in a movie. I was on the other side of the camera, watching these three—a half-Polish girl with an angular nose and long brown hair; a fair-haired, freckled, bulky, excitable Scot; a compact Sudbury-raised Korean with a knowing demeanour, heavy bangs—huddle in a dark booth over this tape recorder, these voices, the idea of their absent friend.

Soundtrack: "This Is the Day," The The. All—almost all—was right with the world. Anything was possible. Ryan and Lee decided to blow off Canadian politics and come with me to the hospital. We took the long way around. Lee had a plan. Flowers for Lou. Not from a stall or vendor or shop, but from the street planters, which were plentiful on the grand boulevard leading to Queen's Park.

"Why don't you just buy some?" asked Ryan.

"It's not the same."

"I get it," I said. I sort of got it. "Lou will appreciate the quest."

Lee nodded.

The wind lashed us when we turned onto University Avenue. We scanned the central median, thick with concrete planters, all clustered around the towering South African monument. The street was grey. The planters were untended, the summer plants either long gone or withering. We stepped up onto benches to see plots of hard, cracked earth littered with chip bags and coffee cups. Several blocks north, in the token landscaping outside a building, we found a smattering of—something. I did not know my flowers very well. What would still be around in early November? Black-eyed Susan? Mums? They were sickly and sparse, but Lee tore a few out of the ground and tucked them, dirt-clumps and all, inside his coat.

On to the hospital. By now it was two o'clock. Lunch had settled. As had our spirits. It was as if we'd suddenly remembered Lou in bed in a hospital room, what this was all about. We crossed the wide boulevard and trudged down the sidewalk in silence.

"GUYS I REALLY APPRECIATE THIS. I DO. BUT I'M SO TIRED." She sent Ryan and Lee away. I walked them into the hallway. I felt responsible.

"I think she had a crap morning. Maybe she didn't sleep much. It's really noisy here."

"Don't worry about it."

"The thing is, you guys would do better cheering her up than me."

"She doesn't want to be cheered up," said Lee.

I watched them walk down the hall. We'd had such fun, in Lou's honour, while she was lying here, what—feeling like shit? Being fussed over by nurses and doctors? Was she now doomed to inspire good times rather than have them?

When I returned to the room, she handed me her journal, that large book with its hard blue cover. This was a signal that I was to read the most recent entry. Then we could delve right into the meat of the matter. Sometimes, this was exciting. Today, though, I didn't want to guess what I'd find. More hand-wringing over Glen? Even more disturbing news on the medical front? She watched me as I turned to the last page of writing. I breathed and let her script fall into focus.

The cat-scans were clear.

Jesus. The CAT scans.

When Dr. Q told us, the three of us, Mom, Dad and me, all started to cry. I get tears just thinking about it. WHAT A RELIEF. I could've had cancer all over me…in my liver or my stomach or my neck—

I looked up. Her eyes glistened. "You didn't really think—"

"I was terrified."

"But you never said—"

"I'm supposed to think positive."

"Says who?"

"I hate being scared. I hate it." Tears were spilling over her eyelids. Her cheeks shone.

We put on the tape I'd brought. I was slouched in a pink, plastic chair beside the bed. She was lying back on the pillows, staring at the perforated tiles on the ceiling, the recorder on her chest, the messages rising as if from within her own self. I noticed the background noise in the recordings. People goofing off. Telling each other what to say. Giggling. Laughing. It all sounded out of place here, like part of a dream world to which she had no access.

"What do you think?"

She smiled. "It's great." But her voice was flat. Her eyes closed.

We sat in silence. It was strange: a lull had fallen over the ward. I heard no beeping equipment, no rolling carts or stretchers, no crackling announcements. Just Louisa's even breaths, and my own. I was reminded of another silence we'd once experienced, in a place that was nothing like this hospital room: it had been cooler, darker, elemental.

"Hey," I said, almost whispering, "remember when we sat in that cave?"

Her eyes didn't open, but she smiled. "God, it was so peaceful."

"It seems like years ago."

"It was only last year. On my birthday."

I slouched deeper, propping my feet on the edge of the chair and hugging my knees close. "You were so angry with me that day."

Her eyelids fluttered open. She looked straight at me. "When? No, I wasn't."

"When everyone left without us."

"Oh, that. I wasn't, not really. I was just scared."

Scared. Right, she'd been scared that day, too—for a completely different reason. And I had taken it personally.

I watched her eyes fall shut, and her breaths deepen. I slipped the recorder from her hands and stood there, half leaning over her, thinking: *I should take it away with me.*

She's so tired that later she might not even remember it. She might say, "I had this weird dream that Spence was singing that song from the Frosted Flakes ads." I'd shrug and say, "How bizarre." And, after a pause, "But maybe not so bizarre. For Spence." And she'd laugh.

Her mouth was closed and her faint eyebrows turned up in the centre, the way they did when she was trying to solve something. I set the recorder on the bedside table, sat back down in the chair, and opened my politics text.

When I left an hour later, she was still asleep.

LOU AND I SAT ON A LEDGE SEVERAL FEET BELOW THE forest floor, our backs against cool, grey rock, not speaking. This was not the sort of open-mouthed cave we'd seen in cartoons. There was no "door" into which a boulder could be shoved. This was a gash in the earth, long and narrow and jagged, cutting through roots and muck and rock. The little room in which we sat was dim and roofless. Through the far-away spindled pine branches, we could see a slash of blue sky. To our left the gash cut deeper. You could follow it, scrambling into a narrow tunnel where you found little heaps of icy, hard-packed snow, hunkered down there even after all these weeks of steaming heat, as if this were winter's hideaway, its secret source.

It was the day Lou turned nineteen, exactly one year before the birthday she'd celebrate in hospital. Her birthday had always marked the end of summer. This year, a bunch of us had borrowed cars from our parents, packed a picnic, and driven in a convoy up Walker's Line, north of Highway 5, into farm country. The city fell away behind us and the broad, fenced fields rose up golden and full. I drove the Pacer, with Lou in the passenger seat and three others crammed in the back. We rolled past acres of corn, fields of wheat, and cows standing in grassy pens, immobile.

We turned onto a gravel lane lined with trees and parked in a haphazard row. We donned knapsacks and walked to the end of the lane, where the Niagara Escarpment rose before us like a wall that has been hacked and chipped and beaten and carved, as if by some mad giant. Up there, on Mount Nemo, were dozens of crevice caves that could be easily explored. A trail zigzagged upward, following the juttings and ledges of rock.

"Don't look down," I said to Lou, who was behind me. She was wearing loafers with a slippery tread. The loafers matched her brown cotton shorts and beige knit tank top. She looked classy, even in flimsy summer wear. How did she do it? Her long pale limbs seemed to glow against the chunky, grey rock. "I wouldn't want to kill you on your birthday."

"Thanks a lot," she panted.

At the top I lifted my arms, pressed my hands onto a ledge of earth and hoisted myself up. The climb had woken up parts of me that I hadn't known were asleep. I felt it settle like a memory into my muscles and bones: a new motion that could be repeated, a small journey fulfilled. I stood before a forest of pines, oaks, and ancient cedars, with its hush and its thick, sweet fragrance, its vast carpet of needles. Up came Lou. Then Esme followed by Adam. Nicky. We waited quietly for the others. You could hear them shouting and laughing, and though they were just over the edge they seemed like voices from another dimension, which is how they seem to me in a different way, now, in memory. A blur of companions who would, within days—when several of us would move away for university, or enter college, or start "real" jobs—disperse into new realities, unknown lives. I watched their faces change, one by one, as they beheld the forest. It was as though the quiet entered us as we entered it.

A short while later I found myself ducking and crouching through an underground tunnel, behind a few of the guys. I could just make out a murmur from above, where the others had remained, sitting on rocks and logs, raising their faces to streams of sunlight cutting through the trees. The tunnel was chillingly damp and darker than night. We might not find our way out; the tunnel might only lead deeper into the earth, sucking us down. But then—yes!—the light at the end, bright deliverance. We emerged through the opening and climbed up onto a soft pine-needle bed. Needles stuck to my palms. I must have been sweating. The tunnel was just a few feet below the surface, but we'd gone under: I'd been in the earth instead of on it.

I tried to convince Lou to try it, but she held up her hands and shook her head: no way. "I saw those caves along the way." She meant the ones that opened right through the wall of the cliff. If you descended into those you'd never come back up; you'd tumble down, knock against craggy rock and tree branches, and land, splotch, in the corn field below.

"It's solid," I told her. "I walked through."

"I'm happy here, thanks."

I was annoyed. Lou could be so bold when it suited her. Where was her sense of adventure, the one she was always claiming to live for? "You have to. It's like nothing you've ever done before." She shook her head.

"What if you regret it? What about Carpe Diem?"

She sighed. "Show me."

We walked to the lip of the crevice and looked over. It wasn't so far down, but the sides were steep.

"I'm going to fall."

"Come on. Follow me."

A few awkward steps on bits of jutting rock and we stood on flat bottom. We were in. The temperature had dropped several degrees. The voices of our friends were gone. She looked at me and grinned.

"See?"

"Mm-hmm."

She sat. I sat. The rock pressed through my T-shirt into the skin of my back. I felt the cold move through me. I closed my eyes.

When I opened them the light had changed to blue-grey and a coolness had settled in my bones. Had I slept? Lou was a few feet off, eyes shut, utterly still: like a figure in ivory, sculpted into the wall of the cave. She opened her eyes and looked my way.

"I could stay here forever."

"We'd need provisions."

"Blankets."

"Boys."

She laughed. I laughed. The spell was broken.

We hauled ourselves to the surface and stood. The forest was darker than when we'd climbed down. And silent.

"They forgot about us."

"Maybe they thought we went ahead."

Lou gave me a look that said *You're always trying to pretend everything's fine when it isn't. It's fucking annoying.*

As if to prove her unspoken criticism true, I pretended not to notice her annoyance. I looked at the sky. When did it get dark these days? "It's getting late. We should go."

"Do you know the way?"

"Yes." Firmly. How could we get lost if we kept the cliff edge to our left? "Follow me." I'd once said the same words, in the same don't-argue-with-me tone, to my little sister, when we couldn't find our parents at MarineLand. "We're lost," she'd cried. I had a map of the park in my head: I could place us precisely in relation to the cafeteria, the petting zoo, the aquarium, the rides. "We're not lost," I told her, gripping her hand tightly, leading her through the crowds, scanning, desperately scanning, for our mother's worried face, our father's dark hair. "I know exactly where we are."

As Lou and I walked back down what I hoped was the way we'd come, I made sure to keep in sight the Blue Trail markers on the trees. We should not veer far from these. I was nervous about those bottomless crevices we'd passed on the way. I watched the ground, alert for openings.

Louisa stopped and stood among the pines, looking left and right, as though a different reality—or one of our friends—might step out from behind a narrow trunk. If you take in all the years before and after this moment, Lou and I must have spent hundreds of hours talking together. Phone calls, sleepovers, wanderings through Burlington, late nights at our co-op, GO trains, cafés, meals. Idle chatter, gossip, study sessions, pep talks, ponderings, confessions. I'm struck at how few of these conversations I explicitly recall, and how many of my memories feature, instead, the two of us in shared silence: such as when I sat by her hospital bed while she slept, or when we sat side by side in the cave. Or when we stood unmoving in the forest, listening, hoping to hear familiar voices.

Lou sighed. "I can't believe they left." This was what you got for taking a risk. She'd gone into the cave—she'd let me talk her into it—and look. She'd been abandoned. I was here, but so what? I was always here.

The sweet smell of soft needles underfoot rose around us. The coolness of the rock in the cave clung to my skin. I was sure—I told myself this—that if we kept walking in the direction we were headed, keeping the escarpment's edge firmly to our left, we would soon find our friends. "Come on," I said, "it's not far."

I was right: after a short hike farther along, we were met at the top of the trail that would lead us back down with a raucous chorus: "There you are!" "We thought you'd gone ahead!" "Why'd you go and scare us like that?"

I grinned at Louisa. "See?"

But she didn't look relieved, or pleased, more like she'd been through a trial she could have done without.

I PLANNED MY EVENING SCHEDULE AS FOLLOWS: HISTORY, English, a quick dinner, back to the hospital. Clear CAT scans or not, Louisa was still stuck there till her infection cleared up and her swollen leg was back to normal. Before leaving our unit, I called to ask what she wanted me to bring. As I jotted a list, she mentioned that her name was spelled wrong on the chart hanging on the end of her bed.

"How'd they spell it? With an *e*? That doesn't inspire confidence."

"It's not a big deal."

"Didn't the nurse last time keep calling you Louise?"

She didn't seem bothered. But I was. Wasn't the medical profession supposed to be precise? Yet they couldn't get the patient's name right? I got out our tin of crayons and drew her name in big colourful letters on a piece of construction paper. I slipped it into one of the binders she'd asked me to bring and grabbed a roll of tape.

I carried two backpacks; the first, laden with Lou's binders and notebooks, was strapped to my shoulders. The other, her small green knapsack, I held by its handles like a shopping bag. Into this sack, as per her instructions, I'd stuffed Lucky the Care Bear, the giant Tweety nightshirt that was a gift from her father (his nickname for her was Tweets), some track pants, and a sweatshirt. She'd only been in the hospital two nights but had already spilled grape juice on all the clothes she'd brought, including *my* camp T-shirt. The clocks had just turned back, and night had fallen early. The hospital entrance to which I was headed was near the end of a poorly lit street with narrow sidewalks. I kept a brisk pace, hugging the curb to avoid the recessed doorways of abandoned shops. I took comfort in the signs nailed to the lampposts: *Quiet! Hospital Zone.*

Lou was on the sixth floor, in a room adjacent to the nursing station. She was sharing with an older woman, who was asleep. Lou motioned for me to be quiet. I firmly taped my homemade nameplate to the end of her bed. Then she led me down the hall to the TV room. We shut the door. We had an agreement with the nurses, who knew all about far-away Glen and Lou's career goals—which lately had to do with hosting her own TV show, à la Valerie Pringle—and even a little about me. So long as we disturbed no one, we were free to ignore regular visiting hours. In here, we could be as noisy as we wanted. Sometimes the nurses came in to see us. If they ordered pizza, they offered us some. I didn't know whether this was normal behaviour for nurses or not. I liked to believe Lou had charmed them, not that they pitied her for being young.

Lou was still wearing the purple-stained T-shirt and pink track pants she'd had on earlier. I'd never seen her in a hospital gown. If she had warning that certain people were visiting, she would ask me to turn the crank at the end of the bed to prop up the mattress behind her back. Then she'd pull her makeup and mirror out of the drawer in the bedside table and get to work. Years later I came to think this effort on her part was not such a bad thing; the careful application of eyeliner, the spinning of the mascara brush, the sweeping of the lip gloss, were a distraction and a grounding. But at the time I wished she didn't care. How she looked wasn't the point.

We could have watched *Roseanne*—there were reruns every half-hour, it seemed, and Lou loved *Roseanne*—but we didn't turn on the TV. Lou had brought the menu sheets with her for the next few days. She sat back on the couch and slid them my way. During her first hospital stay, we'd been delighted to learn that patients could order their own meals. It was still hospital food, but Lou lit up when the menus arrived. In here, you did what you could to make it seem like something, anything, was going on. I took out a pen and, on all three forms, checked off butterscotch pudding under dessert, and cereal for breakfast: those choices never varied. Then I began reading out the main courses for lunch and dinner. Tomato soup. Grilled cheese. She went with chicken for dinner on one day, hot turkey on the next, shepherd's pie on the third.

I couldn't help saying, "It won't be as good as ours." We used creamed corn, always, as the middle layer, and onion soup mix to season the beef.

"I know. But all shepherd's pie is good."

"This is making me hungry." I'd had fish sticks and a salad before walking to the hospital, but it began to feel like I hadn't eaten at all.

"Me too."

I dug in my coat for some change, then we walked down the hall—slowly because of the swelling in her leg—to the elevators. We stepped in and pressed the "down" arrow. We descended and descended. The doors cranked open onto a white hallway. The hospital basement. Somewhere down here was the morgue. I tried not to read the directional signs.

We were headed for a cavernous, low-ceilinged room lit with fluorescent lights, filled with chrome-legged tables and chairs. From it seeped a hum, as from a bank of slot machines. The noise was the product of the juice machines, coffee machines, pop machines, and chip and chocolate bar machines. They lined an entire wall, some a bleak veneer and others painted with rivers of bubbly soda. A few contained carousels on which sat yogurt cups, fruit cups, egg salad sandwiches, crackers and cheese, lone apples and oranges, plastic-wrapped trays of carrot sticks and radishes and celery, granola bars, packs of oatmeal cookies. You could get watery hot chocolate and add a coffee creamer or two to make it taste all right. You could buy a serving of instant soup: a waxed paper cup would pop out of the machine and sit on its grate, propped between metal arms. Through an unseen spout, the machine would spit the steaming broth into the wobbling cup.

This was vending-machine heaven: the sole source of food when the hospital cafeteria was closed. We always found a smattering of shift workers here, sitting at tables in their scrubs, eating stale sandwiches and yogurt with white plastic spoons. The place was an Edward Hopper painting, bleak and overlit, filled with sad faces and unsatisfied hunger.

We stood before a carousel, pressing the button. The wares turned and turned. Louisa stared with an unnerving focus through the smudged glass. In the harsh light, she was all pale skin and shadows, like a hologram version of herself. I pressed my forehead against the machine and peered in at the cups and boxes and bags of food tucked in their cubbyhole shelves. We drew out the moment of decision as long as we could, not wanting to let the green apple go, or leave the cheddar cheese or barbecue chips or any tantalizing possibility behind.

NINE

Subcutaneous Energy

LOUISA STOOD BY THE SINK FULL OF DIRTY DISHES. ON the counter was the frying pan we'd used to cook minute steaks the night before, and a rice pot filled with cloudy water. The cutting board was stained red from tomatoes and littered with crumbs. The paring knife was lying where I'd left it after slicing an apple that morning.

Months had passed, during which Lou's cancer had embedded itself into our routines. Classes, assignments, meals, medical appointments, dishes, a new tumour, pub nights, pills, domestic chores, drug side effects, another new tumour, visits home. That clear CAT scan had been, briefly, a tremendous relief. Good news, for sure. But it had only meant the cancer hadn't migrated to her internal organs. It had nothing to do with these new lumps popping up here and there just beneath her skin.

I'd followed her to the kitchen from her bedroom. We'd been in the middle of a conversation when she remembered she hadn't taken her pill. Levamisole. She was long past taking birth control. Hormones are a no-no when you have cancer: they're like adrenalin for tumours.

In her right hand she held a full glass of orange juice. In her left, a white tablet the size of an aspirin. Her pill-swallowing routine had changed. She raised her head, walked toward the stove, turned, and took five or six paces back toward the fridge. Then she turned back to the stove. Step. Step. Step. Back and forth, three times, four. Finally, she worked up the nerve. She stopped, tilted her head, and opened her mouth. Wide, like a young bird beneath the dangled worm. She dropped in the pill, straight back, and followed it, fast, with three gulps of juice. No chance for the thing to rest on her tongue and send a message to her brain: I am a pill. I will lodge in your throat.

She began to talk, as though we hadn't been interrupted. But I caught a little glimmer of triumph crossing her face. The pill was now somewhere inside her, doing its job. Go, Lou's immune system, go!

"I tried not to cry, but I couldn't help it," she was saying. "Maybe he just didn't get it."

"But he's a yoga guy."

"I know!"

We sat with that for a moment.

Yoga was good for circulation, good for relaxation; it made you strong and it cleared your head of useless thoughts. All useful to a person trying to rally her immune system. It would do her good. Calm her. Calm was what she needed, not all this constant worry.

The yoga class was hard. It might well have been painful regardless. Yoga is not as gentle as it appears: it takes muscle and resilience to hold those poses. But there was a lump now over her right collar bone and another under her left breast, inconveniently exactly where her bra rested, and where the material rubbed when she twisted or turned. Meanwhile, her leg where the lymph nodes had been excised was still not quite right. She'd never had difficulty keeping up with a class in anything; in fact, she seldom had a problem whizzing past her classmates.

This was not the relaxing hour she'd envisioned.

The instructor invited the participants to talk to him after class if they had any special needs. She approached. Her long red hair was pulled back, her lumps and scars hidden beneath her loose T-shirt and jogging pants. She stood before him, a smiling, apparently healthy twenty-year-old. "I have an illness I'd like to talk to you about," she'd said.

He'd chuckled. "It's not life-threatening, is it?"

Her mouth had fallen open. "They...don't know." And then came tears, shocking them both.

"I mean, you'd think he'd be—" I started.

"More sensitive? Aware?"

"Less of a prick."

"He wasn't that bad."

I raised an eyebrow. "How many guys do you think are really interested in yoga, just for their own well-being?"

"Well. He wasn't even cute."

"Hence the Twister."

She laughed.

The yoga teacher worked hard to redeem himself. The following week he handed Lou a worksheet illustrating stretches and movements that she could use in place of any that caused her pain. He told her not to strain herself, to rest as needed, to work at her own pace. She sat in a corner and did almost nothing the rest of the class was doing. He did not ignore her, though. His every word, every movement screamed *I'm sorry. I'm an ass!*

At the doctor's office Lou picked up a pamphlet for Wellspring, a cancer support centre in an old coach house about a fifteen-minute walk from our place, and just down the road from Princess Margaret Hospital. This was the ticket. Adios, regular-people yoga. Sayonara, guilt-ridden guru!

I walked to Wellspring with her. The coach house was charming and cozy, set way back from the road, like a country inn for cancer patients. A plush library. A well-appointed sitting room. Books and videos and classes and counselling. There wasn't just yoga but qigong, tai chi, body-mind meditation. Were there really enough people with cancer to warrant all this? There were. We were part of a booming industry on the fringes of society. I did not find this a comfort, not at all.

The volunteer at the front desk smiled. How could she help? I wondered whether it was obvious to her which one of us was afflicted. Maybe by virtue of being among cancer patients all the time, she could sense it. She told us there was no cost for books or classes or anything. We looked at each other. Could this be?

Louisa asked about peer counselling. The woman explained that this involves being paired with another cancer patient. "You help each other through the challenges," she said, smiling broadly.

I elbowed Lou. "It's like, you get to talk shop."

She signed up for that, as well as yoga. She signed two books out of the library: Dr. Bernie Siegel's *Love, Medicine and Miracles*, and *You Can Heal Your Life* by Louise L. Hay.

The coziness of the place began to cloy. Voices could be heard from behind closed doors. Feet shuffled on the wood floor upstairs. I thought, *Colonel Mustard with a candlestick in the library. Miss Marple suspects the vicar*. Victorian sick rooms and consumption. How many of the people in this house right now would last the year? The month? I thought of Smith's, the funeral parlour in downtown Burlington where Esme's mother had recently been laid out after dying of breast cancer. If that's what it had been by that point. Since that great reprieve in that other life, when we were all still in high school, when she'd seemed to improve, the cancer had turned up in other places, mainly in her back: her spine. It was too aggressive to stop or fix. At the funeral home, Esme wore a jacket and skirt and smiled brightly at all the visitors, taking their hands, as if to assure them that this was no tragedy, her mother wasn't really lying a few feet to the left, her hands folded across her chest. *We're just playing along. Later, don't worry, we'll all go back to normal.* That house and this one, the funeral parlour and Wellspring, exuded the flavour of a similar, bygone era. Ornate mouldings, wainscotting, soft table-lamp lighting, wingback chairs with polished, curving legs.

I wanted out of here. I wanted Louisa out. I didn't want her to feel that she belonged.

LEVAMISOLE WAS AN IMMUNOMODULATOR, A WORD that made it sound as though it wasn't a pill but a piece of machinery equipped with knobs and controls, by which you could reset your whole immune system. Like any improbable invention, it was imperfect, even dangerous. According to the literature Lou was given, it could cause: fever, chills, weakness, nausea, vomiting, diarrhea, anxiety, nervousness, depression, mouth sores, loss of appetite, stomach pain, change in taste or smell, muscle or joint pain, fatigue, dizziness, headache, and skin rash.

There was, as yet, no internet with which to look this stuff up. We didn't know that levamisole was most commonly prescribed to people with colon cancer, and only helped a fraction of them get better. I found this out years later via Wikipedia. Nor that, when recommended to melanoma patients, it was usually coupled with a poor prognosis—and, in such cases, was more likely to work on people over fifty-five.

The list of side effects was disturbing enough. Fever? Depression? Mouth sores? Maybe this was as bad as chemotherapy. Maybe worse. I asked Lou, "Where would you draw the line? How would you decide whether it was still worth it? Would you even know it was working? What if your decision was tainted by depression caused by the drug? How could you even trust your own feelings?"

She looked at me like she wanted me to shut up.

She went to Burlington on a Friday to spend the weekend with her mother, and came back Sunday night, exhausted and elated. She'd spent the evening trapped in her bedroom on the third floor of the townhouse, trying to escape the smell of dinner cooking, which made her want to puke. Levamisole was somehow recalibrating her nose. "I'll never eat a pork chop again," she said, pulling a face.

While holed up in her room, she'd opened the book by Louise L. Hay, hoping for distraction. "It's amazing. She says you can *do* this. You can use your mind to affect what's happening in your body."

Her face was flushed. Was this one of the side effects? Hypertension? Hysteria? The book was in her hand. She gripped it by the spine, waving it about as she spoke. She could do this. She could make herself well, just by the power of her mind.

Visualization. That's what it was hinged on. By now I understood that meant imagining scenes inside the body, dramatic scenes that involved the dissolution of the cancer cells. What did the cancer cells look like? Whatever you wanted. Whatever you decided. You were in charge. I'd picked up the Siegel book one day, while Lou was out. It fell open to some glossy illustrations in the middle. There, next to a childish drawing of a woman sitting in a chair, with a spider on her chest and a black object pointing into the palm of her hand, was a caption explaining that the woman was not giving her whole self to the problem. That she'd drawn her disease in the form of an insect was not positive enough. Colouring her treatment black was likewise negative. Worse, the treatment was pointing at her body rather than going inside. The conclusion: because she'd failed to "accept"—it's not explained what exactly—she'd likely also fail to get well.

I flipped a few pages further, to a drawing of a person lying on a table under a blue machine. From it emanated purple and yellow rays, entering the person's body at the correct places: making direct contact with the disease. The patient was accepting her therapy (even deep within her unconscious mind), displaying hope and a positive attitude toward her treatment.

I went on. A picture of a sad woman holding a purple syringe was described as illustrating how the patient was honest about her misgivings, but unconsciously willing to receive treatment (purple is spiritual, and the figure's feet turn toward the needle). Her fears receded, and her tumours followed suit.

I tried to tell myself this made sense. Why shouldn't the mind be this strong? Why shouldn't you be able to harness it to your advantage? What if we all visualized on Louisa's behalf? It could be like having nuns in a convent pray for you. Sending the saint to God as your emissary, presenting your plea.

But part of me was thinking, Right, okay, how's this for visualization: *I'm myself and Louisa's herself, and we sit as we*

are right now, on her bed in our student co-op. I grab the book
from her hand and crank open the window. A breath of cold air
rushes in, reminding us of the rest of the world and all the things
going on out there, how much we cannot hope to control. I throw
the book out, not caring about the prostitutes down there, or
anyone who might be walking by. The silence, our stillness, our
listening, is almost visible, something solid and green, an undis-
turbed field, a towering, stoic old pine.

After a long moment, we hear the thud.

It was February, but it wasn't so cold. It was unseason-
ably mild. Of course, I didn't grab the book. I threw nothing
out the window. Instead, I was saying to Lou, What do you
want me to visualize? What would be best?

TOGETHER, LOU AND I ATTENDED AN ODD MIX OF CONCERTS
over the years: the Cure, John Cougar Mellencamp, the
Psychedelic Furs, U2, Billy Joel. I'd love to claim that this
weirdly random list suggests our complex tastes in music.
But really, it was chance. Like everyone else, we were at the
mercy of Ticketmaster, a bit stunned each time we managed to get a call through before all the tickets for a given
concert were gone. Success required a redial button, quick
reflexes, and old-fashioned luck. The concerts, thrilling
as they were, eventually blurred into vague memories of
pounding music, disorienting light displays, and crowds. I
do remember Billy Joel's red socks flashing along the dark
floor as his fingers flew over the piano keys.

More vividly than any concert, I recall the night we went
to see a famous author-doctor deliver his message of mind-
body connection to a packed house at a downtown Toronto
theatre. No music, no dancing, no feverish thrill.

That's the show that marked me.

We sat near the back of the theatre. Between us and the bald man on stage, row upon row of cancer patients sat with husbands or wives, children and grandchildren, boyfriends, girlfriends, or just plain old friends like me. I noticed the headscarves, wigs, and canes weaving up and down the aisles, the bodies they were connected to, the bone-thin arms and sallow cheeks. Lou sat next to me straight and tall, her hands folded in her lap. Her thick red hair was tied back. How many people here coveted that hair? Cursed her for having it?

Walking back and forth across the stage with a microphone in his hand, the author was sharing the story of a former patient who'd told him it was all well and good to go see the doctor, but what was she supposed to do in between appointments? How was she meant to live? The question, he declared, had changed his life. Until that moment he hadn't considered the life of the cancer patient outside his office.

It was difficult not to warm to this story. The man was admitting his own failure, after all. The reason he'd shaved his head, he told us, was to display solidarity with his patients. But the more he described his self-transformation, the more wary I felt. He seemed so very pleased with this new understanding he'd found.

I was well aware of the irony of my skepticism in the face of this man's message of optimism and hope. When he launched into a visualization exercise, I was determined to give it a whirl, to really, honestly try. I closed my eyes and listened.

Eyes closed. Back straight. Chin up. Feet still. Arms relaxed. Breathe in. Breathe out.

So far, so good. It was like that delicious few moments at the end of gym class when the teacher would get you all to lie on the floor and work up from the toes—relax, relax! We were kids, maybe eight or nine years old. Row upon row lying face-up on the old gym floor. We wore bright T-shirts and red faces—from recent exertion—and faint smiles. We felt safe, enrobed in the teacher's lulling voice. It was the only time in school that I was ever able to forget the people around me and what they might be thinking.

The memory had presented itself to me, so I went with it. I began to visualize a vast gymnasium full of children, quiet children, row upon row of them, lying on the floor, relaxing their fingers and toes, free from the anxiety of the class-room or the torments of the playground, mesmerized by a kind, distant, soothing voice.

Deep. Deeper. Now. Concentrate. Draw the picture in your mind—the colours, the shapes, the movement. Let your world dissolve into the image. Feel its positive energy. Feel the calm. The hope. The healing.

I opened my eyes. How does one manufacture positive energy? Really?

I looked over at Lou. Her eyes were shut firm, her mouth a determined line. The cut of her pale face was elegant, her nose gently upturned. But. But! There in front of her pretty, seashell ear, caught just below her jaw as though it had shimmied up the tendons of her neck: the newest rock-hard mound of mutant cells. A subcutaneous node, they called this in the lingo. You wanted to rub it clean, brush it away.

When Louisa went to see Dr. Q, he'd pull out a measuring tape, divided into millimetres—similar, I imagined, to one used by a seamstress. He laid it flat against the lump in her arm, the one on her chest nestled in among her ribs, and now this new one, higher up. He jotted down the figures. Then they sat down together with his notes to compare with the previous month's results. Back at our place she'd share the news, whether the tumours were growing or shrinking. It was like a pass or fail report. If they'd gone down, it wasn't just relief and hope; it was success. Louisa the good student. Louisa kicking the shit out of the disease.

If they'd gone up, as they had this week—just a couple millimetres here and there—well.

"I keep letting myself think negative thoughts. I get scared. I can't help it."

I waited for the bestselling author-doctor to address this problem, of how easily this hope-inspiring system of his might breed guilt and shame. The way I saw it, he owed me a little guidance, a little help. While he was down there in the spotlight telling happy stories of "survival," I was way up here in the cheap seats—which weren't so cheap for a couple of cash-strapped students—dealing with their implication.

Perhaps it was all misconstrued by Louisa, and by me. This wasn't the way it was meant to work. But how then? How did you judge your success or failure at mind-body influence—at *fighting cancer*—if not by the fluctuating size of the lump in your neck?

It's within this family of memories that my anger still rears, as I recall Louisa's struggle to live up to not just her own expectations of herself, but also those embraced by the culture around the disease. I'm defensive on her behalf about the framing of cancer as a "battle." I resent the metaphor for the pressure it places on people who are ill—flailing, confused, terrified. Their own bodies have, in a sense, turned against them. "Fighting" cancer, by implication, means fighting themselves.

I wished I'd sat on the other side of Lou in the theatre, because I kept glancing sidelong at her neck. I hated the word *survivor*, its smugness. I hated the lump, all those cells that had joined forces and boldly settled, like the suitors in

The Odyssey, eating up the best sheep and poisoning the characters of the servants—or, in this case, the healthy cells. I did understand the appeal of the author's message: the sense of taking control when control seems all but out of reach. But it was hard to believe that tumour took even passing notice of the extraordinary effort, both mental and emotional, Louisa was putting into its destruction.

What vibrant image was Lou devising? I could feel her effort like a circling of dust in the air, making it vivid and symbolic and true, and I thought, You can't discount these claims regarding the power of the mind. Look at her. This was Louisa all over, rallying for life. *You are no longer welcome here!* That's what she was saying to the lump. Shouting at it. A team of wolves were chasing it off the mountain. It was a weasel. A jackal. Mangy and corrupt.

But it sat unmoved, hovering below her chin, defying gravity and common decency, for all we knew already infiltrating the tissue around it. I could almost hear it growl.

TEN

Blood Work

I LET MY EYES FALL TO THE SMUDGED TILES ON THE FLOOR, to the brown tasselled loafers and ratty sneakers, the scuffed beige pumps and desert boots and dumpy Hush Puppies and the one pair of polished brown brogues. The shoes were tucked under the chairs; they rocked and rocked, crossed and uncrossed, tapped and tapped. People weren't even whispering. Was it the air? The colourless walls? Maybe, just now, as I blinked, an extra wrinkle appeared on that man's forehead. One hair follicle fell into grey.

This was our second holding room of the day at Princess Margaret Hospital. The chairs lining the walls, an alcove off a busy hallway, were full. We stayed near the desk, on our feet. In the first, we'd waited an hour for a nurse to call Louisa in and prick her thumb for blood. Then a quick bowl of too-salty chicken noodle soup in the basement cafeteria: we crushed our soda crackers inside the plastic wrappers and dumped the crumbs into the broth.

I looked at Louisa, leaning against the unattended desk. There was no outward sign of the distress her body was in.

The lump just below her left breast alternately leaked puss, scabbed, cracked open, and bled. The one lower down her midriff interfered with her belt. The one lodged beneath a muscle in her back caused almost constant pain, which she tried to keep down with Tylenol 3s. For months, until she finally received the results from an MRI, this pain had her convinced the cancer had infiltrated her spine or one of her lower organs. A kidney? The bottom of a lung? But no, it was just one more lump, in a particularly inconvenient place. When she told me, I was so happy I almost began to cry. It's just another tumour. Hooray!

We were here for her latest treatment: a form of chemo-therapy. Every three weeks she'd come here three days in a row for IV administration of the medication, but if her platelet count was too low—meaning her system had weak-ened too much to take the drugs—she'd be sent home, and the whole routine would begin again the following day. The dreariness stretching out before her, of all the time to be spent in rooms such as this, was, to me, an egregious affront. She had a life to live, my friend, and this most definitely was not it.

IT WAS SEPTEMBER 1992, A YEAR AFTER HER DIAGNOSIS, and this—the chemo—her third line of attack. The levamisole had seemed promising, but then her tumours resumed grow-ing. The treatment was stopped in favour of Interleukin-2, a drug based on a natural protein that already exists in the body. The Interleukin worked by marking the presence of a foreign body (i.e., a tumour) and stimulating the growth of T-cells and Natural Killer Cells—what a satisfying name for them!—and then sending them, like a band of thugs, to do away with the intruder. Lou's Interleukin was administered in hospital, by intravenous, over several hours a shot. Side effects were nearly non-existent, which made the whole effort seem promising.

But one day she came home from a doctor's appointment, to which she'd gone with her mother, and told me Interleukin was out, chemotherapy in.

What is this? Three strikes and you're out?

It will make her sick.

This is it, the real thing.

"For how long?" I asked.

Lou shrugged. "Until it works."

Multiple-agent chemotherapy, they called it. It was a cocktail of several drugs—Cisplatin, Dacarbazine, and BCNU—none of which I knew anything about. I'd been surprised to learn that chemo wasn't just chemo; there were dozens of mixtures and some of them weren't so bad when it came to side effects. Also, there was now something you could take—yet another pill—to combat the nausea.

The next time I went to Burlington for a weekend I noticed a book leaning on my shelf that I remembered reading several times as a girl. Called *Michelle*, it was the "true" story of a girl who'd lost a leg to cancer, just like Terry Fox. Only, unlike Terry Fox, she'd survived—at least as far as the writing of this book. I pulled it down. On the back cover was a picture of the girl. I was taken aback by how familiar it seemed. How much time had I spent staring at it, wanting to know to this girl? She was thin and willowy, wearing a halter top, long black pants, and cowboy boots. The stump of her right leg was propped on the handgrip of a crutch, giving her balance while she tied a harness around a horse's neck. Her hair was short, and a wisp of bangs flew up, caught in a breeze.

I began flipping pages. I was sure the part when Michelle was on chemo had been horrific and that that, perversely, had been part of the book's appeal—what made her a hero. I skimmed what now seemed like wooden dialogue, too much sweetness between the girl and her parents, and a lot of talk about Jesus and prayer. Finally, in the chapter called "A Newborn Sparrow," I found it. Fever, chills, and puke. Phrases such as "violently ill" and "sieges of trembling." The girl couldn't bear sunlight. It hurt her eyes, so drapes were always pulled.

Dry mouth, I thought now, the book didn't mention that. Nor a throat so sore it hurts to swallow.

WE FINALLY FOLLOWED THE NURSE THROUGH THE DOUBLE doors. Lou was saying, "This is Lillian. She was on shift last time I came in."

Lillian was tall and starched, her face taut. She brusquely shook my hand. "It's so nice of you to come in with Louisa." I fixed my eyes upon her. *I'm not doing her a favour, lady. I want to be here. I like it here.*

She left us at a bed across from the nurse's headquarters. The room was large and partitioned, with blue drapes affixed to tracks in the ceiling. Most of the drapes were partly pulled back, and in the spaces behind them people sat in vinyl reclining chairs or were lying in bed. Beside them were wheeled racks with small clear sacs of liquid dangling from metal hooks. Tubes ran from the sacs into arms or other body parts. Some people were alone, and some were not. Some were watching television. Others had closed their eyes. There was little sound save the rustle of nurses and the low murmur from the TV sets. When you are surrounded by bodies attached to tubing, something shifts beneath you. Years later, watching the film *The Matrix*, I would remember this room when regarding the eerie scene in which the machines' secret is revealed: rows of liquid-filled pods in which living humans floated, attached to the wires that drew from them their heat and energy, while their simulated selves existed in a simulated world.

Lou and I sat on the edge of the bed, side by side. Lillian returned, exuding an even higher level of efficiency.

"Your platelets are very low, you know. Who told you it was okay?"

"They were okayed by Dr. Q. It's fine. Really. They're way up from last week."

She was dangerously near tears. We'd already been in the hospital more than three hours. Louisa had braced herself for the pinprick blood test, the boredom, the coldness of the chemo fluid running through her. Now Nurse Lillian was on the verge of sending her home without a single drop of treatment.

"I'll have to double-check with the nurses at the desk," she said, with unexpected gentleness. "I just have to be sure." She patted Lou on the shoulder and marched off. It occurred to me she was just doing her job. And doing it thoroughly.

"We'll never get out of here before four," said Lou. "I'm sorry. You didn't have to come."

"It's okay."

"Will you get to work on time?"

Probably not. But it didn't matter.

"But we'll have to wait another half-hour before they even start." Her anxiety was building. "And then it takes an hour and a half. I don't want to—" She broke off. She smiled broadly, looking past me. "Hey! Here comes Tanya."

I turned and saw Tanya, the nurse who kept close track of all Dr. Q's patients, walking toward us with a thick folder under her arm. Her hair was pulled back into an elastic. Smiling, she waved.

"It's all cleared up, Louisa. Now wipe that scowl off your face!"

"I was wondering when you were going to show up," Lou said, wrapping her arms around her knees. I stood, expectant. Our gloom had lifted.

"Well, come on. I wouldn't miss your first chemo of the month. How are you feeling?"

"Not bad."

"Are you eating?"

"I was okay till last week." Last week, her problem with smell, which had been bad enough on the levamisole, had returned fivefold. When any of us were cooking she would hide in her room with the door shut, just in case. "It's not so bad. I just miss getting excited about food." Something we did together. Or used to. Anticipate the food. Eat it—thoroughly, with commitment. Recall it with emphatic statements. I had noticed my own appetite dwindling. I'd lost four pounds since Lou started chemo.

Tanya's beeper went off. She examined it and ran off, promising to return. On the narrow table beside Lou's bed sat the bulky file she'd brought with her, forgotten. "Is that all stuff about you?"

"I guess."

"But it's so thick!"

She shrugged. She was watching Lillian approach with some bags of clear liquid and a tray. I craned my neck to see its contents: crooked tools, bits of tubing and needles. "Here we go." She deftly hung the bags from the wheeled metal post that waited beside the bed. She set the tray on the table, beside Lou's file. "Sorry about the mix-up. Let's get you set, so you and your friend can go home before morning."

Lou winced and leaned back into the pillow. "I hate this part."

Lillian sifted through the needles on the tray. Louisa bent her head to peer at her collar bone. Beneath it was a catheter, with an access tube leading directly into one of her veins. Its shape could just be discerned beneath the skin, as though a miniature spaceship had lodged there. It looked painful to me, a caught thing pressing against the skin, but Lou told me she hardly noticed it.

When she'd started on the Interleukin, which was also administered intravenously, Lou was advised to have the catheter surgically inserted. The extra operation would be less unpleasant in the long run than the prospect of nurses plunging needles here and there in search of a fresh vein. Veins of cancer patients are prone to rebel against the constant intrusion; they shrivel up and close off, making each session more and more of a trial. When Louisa explained this to me, it sounded ghastly. I thought it might be this ritual stabbing that would ultimately break a person down. The sore, needle-mottled arm; the miserable, frustrated nurse.

The catheter wasn't without its discomforts. Once it's accessed, treatment is hassle-free, like opening a lid and pouring in the fluid. But first the skin over the catheter must be pierced, with a tiny needle that looks suspiciously like a thumbtack. A swift movement, but the pain is sharp. It was through a selection of these thumbtacks that Lillian searched. She raised one to the light. Lou bit her lip and gripped the sides of the bed. Lillian lowered the needle to the ridged area above the collarbone where the catheter sat. She positioned it, and then pressed down hard with the heel of her thumb.

Louisa winced. "It hurts!"

"Just think how easy it will be tomorrow." Lillian turned to me and explained that she would cap off the tiny needle so it could be reused for the next two days. Then it would be removed until the next session, in three weeks.

Lou interrupted. "It doesn't usually hurt like this. It doesn't feel right."

Lillian leaned forward to take another look. "It seems fine to me." The hint of a question. "But you know, it didn't go in as easily as it should have." She shook her tray. "Here," she said, holding up a needle that looked, to me, just like the first. "Let's try this."

She leaned over and pulled out the first pin. Louisa winced again as it slid out. "This one won't be so bad," and before Louisa could respond, she'd punched it in. "There. How's that."

"Better."

"Good. Then we're on our way."

Now Lillian was in a hurry. She attached tubes from the bags of liquid to the opening in the catheter. One bag is drugs, she quickly explained, the other is saline, for dilution. She picked up her tray. "I'll be back to switch bags." And dashed away.

I watched her bustle past the other patients, all attached to bags of liquid, the bags going down, the bodies filling up. Some of the liquid was clear, like Lou's. Some was red. Beneath one of these was a woman with a bright scarf tied around her head. "The red stuff makes you lose your hair," Lou said, following my gaze. "They don't use that kind for melanoma."

I turned from the woman in the scarf to Lou, her thick red curls. I retrieved some of the sense I'd had before, when she was a cancer patient who didn't need chemo: that she was on a different plane. She wasn't down in the pit with all the other cancer patients, not yet.

We turned on Oprah, who was talking about girls who drop out of school. We couldn't concentrate; we shut it off.

My eyes fell on the only other thing: Lou's file. "Are you allowed to read it?"

"Of course I can. It's my file." She hauled it across the bed. It was fatter than the illustrated Bible my parents kept on a bookshelf. Only the pages weren't gilded.

Page one: a spotty printout, obviously from an old dot-matrix, of a document dated 1984. We looked at each other. The year Lou was twelve. The year of the cyst. Holy shit. We began to skim. Our eyes were drawn to three words in the last sentence on the page: *possible malignant melanoma.* I tried to go back and read the whole letter but couldn't understand the jargon. Those three words seemed the only ones that could matter anyway.

Lou turned the page. Again, glaring from the jumble of text: *possible malignant melanoma.* That phrase. On the next page, again. And on the next. Each memo was dated that same year, but on a different day. Each was signed by a different doctor. Pathology reports on a cyst that was removed from her shoulder eight years ago.

"Did anyone ever say anything?"

"No. I don't know." She shook her head. No, no, no.

Was there any point, now, in remembering the hours she'd spent in the sun during high school, without sunscreen, on purpose? Was there any point in revisiting her decision to use birth control? I drew the conclusion then that Lou's parents, doctors, or all of them, after discussing it together, had chosen not to worry her about a diagnosis that was only "possibly" true, and that she could do nothing about. She was only twelve, after all. But now I understand she may have known information she never told me—perhaps for fear of making it seem more real, perhaps to avoid seeing the equivalent of her own fear flash across *my* face—or she may have technically known but then not known, ignored or buried the knowledge.

Lou grabbed a thick chunk of pages and turned. We were now deep in the file, very near the present. The pages were handwritten, as a log, and signed by Tanya. Their dates coincided with her checkups, her operations, her follow-up visits. We start to read one dated a few months back. *The cancer is definitely progressing…Louisa is feeling tired and discouraged…the treatment has stopped working…her outlook right now is poor.*

This was Tanya, the nurse Lou had so brightened upon seeing earlier, who had magically cleared up the problem with the platelets, and who never failed to cheer her, to make her feel that things were going well and would improve. Before sitting down to write these logs in private—in secret, it now seemed—she would say the most encouraging things out loud. *You're young and healthy, Louisa. You're doing fine. You've got plenty of options.* That was always a winner. *There's lots we can do, loads we haven't tried. Don't worry. Keep doing what you're doing. Live your life.*

"I'm getting cold." She let her head fall back on the pillow. I unfolded the heavy blankets at the bottom of the bed and piled them on top of her, up to her neck. One, two, three. They weighed a tonne.

"Thanks," she said. "That's good." She closed her eyes. She slept.

I lifted the file from her lap to mine. I flipped back to the middle, somewhere. Typed reports from various nurses, those, I guessed, who were on shift when Lou was in hospital for this or that operation. Similar to Tanya's, they described her disposition, what pain she complained of, her overall health. These, though, were more formal. I could feel the difference, that these nurses didn't know her; she was one among dozens of patients moving through the ward in a given week. The reports were consistent, though. Back pain was always mentioned, insufficient painkillers. Adjectives such as *optimistic* and phrases such as *positive attitude* appeared frequently. I skimmed and there they were. There they were again. *Optimistic. Positive. Positive. Optimistic.* What did they know? Was it better for her, or better for them, if that was what they saw?

I shut the massive file and sat there with it on my thighs, pinned, watching Lou sleep, the liquid in the bag slowly, slowly, slowly going down.

ELEVEN

The Plant Defending Its Stores

THE CACTUS ROOM AT ALLAN GARDENS WAS A LANDSCAPE from another planet. I was staring at the ghost cactus. It grew almost fern-like, with light blue-green arms beneath a white dust. Compared to the beefy, stocky specimens nearby, some of them studded like weapons, it seemed frail, as though it might give in to a sturdy breeze.

"It looks out on the lake," Lou said. She had come up soundlessly beside me. This room was so hot and dry that somehow even movement lost its solidity; I felt that if I lifted a foot it might dissolve. "Huge windows. A wall of windows. It sounds amazing. You can stay whenever you want."

"Thanks."

"Seriously. I won't be far away."

"You should do it. It makes sense."

"I'm sorry."

"Sorry for what?" It came out sharply, which I hadn't intended. I began to feel heady. It had been a good hour since we'd walked into this steamy, glass-encased universe. "I can't believe we've never come here," I said. I needed to change the subject.

Lou nodded too readily. "I know. It's only a block away."

It hit me how much farther away than that her new place would be.

FILLING A VAST CITY BLOCK AND TRAVERSED DIAGONALLY by broad paths lined with mature oak and maple and cherry trees, the park the greenhouses called home was once genteel and pastoral, that was obvious. But it had declined. It was littered now, seedy, the grass patched, the bushes unkempt. Nonetheless, at the west end of the park was this glorious Victorian observatory. That, at least, had not been neglected. And you could just wander in. No charge.

The outing had been a last resort. We'd been sitting in the kitchen, oppressed by dirty dishes and an unswept floor. Crumbs and dust stuck to our socks; they sat on the grey floor like an indictment, bits of matter eyeballing us with disdain. Lou'd been stuck indoors for three days, tired and nauseous and sleepless, but just what could she manage? Unlike a film, or even a conversation in a café, the greenhouses at Allan Gardens somehow demanded less. One could have a look-see, leave a few moments later, and something would have been done, the day altered.

It began to rain as we circled the building, looking for the main entrance. We ducked through an open side doorway. The room we found ourselves in contained two narrow pathways barely passable between rich greenery. The air was thick with moisture. Vines dangled. The bases of palm trees were blanketed with orchids and other brilliant blooms. A replica mill operated along one glass wall, the slowly turning wheel dumping bucketfuls of water into a stream that we crossed in a few steps over an arching footbridge. Jabbed into the ground amid the trunks and foliage were little signs bearing Latin names for the flora. I was struck by their beauty, dismayed that I'd likely forget them all. I turned to Lou. "Why did nobody teach us Latin?"

But she was already gliding into the next greenhouse.

I followed. It was brighter here, the ceiling higher, the trees tall and twisted. Fat goldfish swam in a stonewalled pond. "Look," Lou said, hushed. Water lilies. A gardener in work clothes and muddy boots. Pungent, freshly dug earth.

We moved on, into a round, domed chamber. Palm branches stretched lazily overhead, creating a feeling of enclosure, though the ceiling here was very high, as in a cathedral. Rain ran down the glass walls. Trees with scaly trunks wound about each other like snakes. Everything held the promise of a slither or a wave. We sat on a bench along the path, and I looked around, watching for movement.

Louisa was speaking. The words came slowly, as if from under a matted bed of ferns.

"I think I have to move."

"You mean get up?" We'd only just sat down.

"No." Her hands gripped the front slat of the bench on either side of her knees. "I need to be with my mom."

I didn't get it.

"You know how we had lunch yesterday, after chemo?"

Uh-huh.

"Well, she's moving. She's bought a condo at Harbourfront."

This was a shock. "She's leaving Burlington?"

"And the boys are going to live with Dad."

"When did all this—"

"It's all come up really fast. But it's good. I think they could all use the change."

She would have told me all this last night, but I was out at the pub with Ryan and the guys. When I got home, I didn't knock on her door in case she was finally getting some rest. That tumour in her back pressed painfully into her spine; it wouldn't let up. She often got up in the night to try to walk it off. It was our third year in the co-op, and we had reduced to a four-bedroom unit. Casey was still with us, and our new fourth was Rudy, a pal from journalism who was always game for a late-night tea and chat. The bedrooms ringed the common room and everything seemed smaller than in the larger units, but cozier. It felt like family, only better: camaraderie and intimacy minus all the headaches.

When Lou couldn't sleep she'd tell me the next day, and I would feel bad. I couldn't imagine anything more lonely than being up in the night, suffering. I would tell her she should wake me for company. But to wake a person seems such a violation that you do it only out of absolute desperation. So, in a way, I was glad she never did, because it was a comfort to know it wasn't as bad as that.

That's what I told myself.

"And Mom needs a break," Lou was saying. "She really does."

"But you?"

She looked at me, pleading. *Don't try to talk me out of it. Don't be hurt.* "She'd be all alone."

"It's not your job to take care of her."

"It's not just that. When I'm up at night, and sore, I get thinking—"

"You should wake me. I've told you!" I didn't mean to admonish her.

"I know. I just—I can't."

What I should have said is: *I've let you down. I've been out at the pub, acting like everything's normal.* But it wasn't that simple. Mostly, Louisa wanted normal. Or that's how she let on. It depended on the day, on her mood, on how well the painkillers were working.

She was now working in the cosmetics department at Eaton's, a job for which she wore a long white lab coat open over a skirt and blouse. She'd told me recently that her boss wouldn't let her sit on a stool during her shift, even when she was really fatigued. "You're supposed to stand all the time."

"You can't even take five?"

"Apparently not. It's not like I'm lazy. It's just a little concession. I mean, this isn't frivolous. I have cancer."

But she didn't look sick. And she didn't really want to be treated like a sick person. If she got too many questions about how she was doing in that tone people reserve for the less fortunate, she would avoid the culprit, pretend to be out when they called, and "forget" to call them back. "It's like, some people think you get cancer and everything else stops. That's all there is. They just don't get it."

I tried to judge from day to day: Is she Sick Louisa? In need of a little extra care? Or is she Normal Louisa, Don't Treat Me Like Cancer Girl, I Have a Life? Maybe I'd guessed the latter too many times. It was more appealing as a default position, after all. Cancer? What cancer? We had things to do, people to see.

"You really want to move?"

"It's not that I don't want to be with you guys. It's just. I don't know. When you're sick—"

"You want your mom."

She put a hand over her face. She was pressing tears back in. I touched her shoulder.

"Hey, of course you do." I didn't want my mom when I was sick. I didn't like being fussed over. Had I ever really been sick, though? Not like this.

Finally, her hand dropped. Her face was pink and tight. She sighed. "Don't think—"

"I'm not. Don't worry." But I was. How could I not? I pointed to a doorway across the room. "Let's go in there. Can you?"

We walked around the swirling trees and down a little passage where the moisture seemed to be sucked right out of the air. The rainforest receded and the desert rose before us, arid and parched.

"These are all types of cactuses? There are that many?"

"Cacti. That's how you say it in plural."

I raised an eyebrow. "Really?"

She tried to hide a little smile. If either of us was a stickler for grammar and spelling it was me. It was like she'd scored a point.

Some *cacti* were flat, some were round, some could have fit in a doll house. Others were as tall and thick as trees. This one bloomed huge red flowers, that one delicate pink petals. One grew in long tendrils, like a spider. But the actual "spider cactus" was shaped like a little pumpkin, or an acorn squash. A pretty pink flower, almost like a chrysanthemum, lay open, layered and luxurious, atop a thick stem rising from its core. The name must have come from the veins on the squash-like body, like little white spiders crawling around.

We walked slowly, trancelike. Lou was moving out. I'd failed to provide the necessary comfort. I grew thirsty. The enchantment of the cacti wore off. They seemed to be mocking us, holding all the water, and whatever else they contained, in their secret compartments. They were like growths, giant warts—and, one couldn't help but think, tumours.

One tiny plant grew a little red tuft, like a cotton ball. I reached out.

"Anita, no!"

But I'd already rubbed my finger over it.

"It's okay. It's soft."

"Really?"

We took a few steps. My finger where I'd touched the bloom began to tingle, and then to prick, like it was being stabbed by tiny, invisible swords, a hundred at a time.

"Ow! Fuck."

"You're hurt," Lou said.

I showed her. "Look at them all. They're like stingers." I held my finger up to the dim daylight coming in through the rain and glass. Between the swirling grooves of skin I saw little red flecks, like blood rising. They were cactus prickles, the plant defending its stores.

"They won't last forever." But she sounded dubious.

You're leaving, I thought. *I'm injured, and you're going away*. Tears welled, though the pain was not so great, and far, far away in the tip of a finger. She turned from my hand to my face. The lump in her neck, the only one you could casually notice, seemed to hold still as the rest of her moved, as though it were the axis, the sun. There was no way my stung finger compared; it didn't come close. But in her concern, she had forgotten it. Her eyes were on me. She was herself.

AFTER LOUISA MOVED IN WITH HER MOM, I COPIED MY key for her. That way, between classes, she could come up to the unit for a snooze, a cup of tea, whatever. My bed was her bed, my food her food. In a way, the move was an improvement. She had a sanctuary now, down by the lake with her mother, but she came to our unit often, still part of the "family." It was nice. A pressure had lifted, on both sides.

One day I was grilling a cheese sandwich when she burst into the kitchen. I turned from the stove. She dropped her green knapsack on the table.

"Hey! Great timing. I'll make you a sandwich."

"No thanks."

"You should eat," I said, turning back to the sizzling bread in the pan.

"I can't."

"You need to eat. Even half a sandwich. You love grilled cheese." I sounded like my grandmother.

"Anita."

"Here." I flipped the sandwich. The cooked side was crisped brown, dark, as we liked it. "We can share this one. I'll halve it with the spatula."

"Anita!"

I turned, the plastic spatula raised. "What?"

"I—" She paused. Her mouth fell shut. Then I remembered. Shit.

"You saw the doctor."

She nodded. Her mid-chemo progress report. The measuring tape would have come out, absolutely, for sure. I opened my mouth, then it closed too. We stood there in the kitchen, a few feet apart, the spatula, our unopen mouths, and the sizzle of the grilling sandwich between us.

She was pale as flour. Her eyes swam. I gripped the spatula more tightly.

"Oh my God, what?"

"They're shrinking."

"Huh?"

"He checked them all."

"Holy shit."

Holy shit. But hang on. I had heard this before. There had been shrinkage with the levamisole, and then the Interleukin. Initial shrinkage. The sandwich was probably done. "But, you mean—"

"No, I mean, they're really shrinking. Dramatically. He says he's never seen it work so quickly. He said, 'I hesitate, but I think we can almost use the word…'"

Spit it out. Come on. Spit it out.

"We can *almost* say remission."

By the *mish* in mission, in a trance, without taking my eyes off her—she didn't look sick; she never had, just a little thinner—I reached back across the stove and clicked off the element. I dumped the spatula on the counter.

Now my hands were free. I placed them on her shoulders. "Really?" In a tiny voice. Any moment one of us might fall to the floor and wake up. Eating was out of the question.

"The school?"

"Let's go."

It was my third year in the journalism program, Lou's second in Radio and Television Arts. By then, the old journalism building had been abandoned. Our two programs were headquartered in a new building with a vast central hall, high-tech production studios, and newsrooms equipped with wide-screened Macs. Wordlessly, an invisible force holding us abreast, we marched into the RTA student lounge, stopped inside the doorway, and scanned the room. Anyone here? Anyone we knew? Anyone who cared? Journalism lounge next. Then the third-year reporting class we knew to be underway. Within an hour we'd held hushed conferences in quiet corners all over the building. At benches, over keyboards, on the thresholds of our favourite professors' offices, in the computer-clogged *Ryersonian* newsroom, where we caught Ryan with the *Canadian Press Stylebook* open on his lap, checking copy.

"Hey!" He thought I was paying a friendly girlfriend visit. But I didn't speak. Neither did Louisa. He got spooked. "What is it? What?" Standing, the open book falling, his jeans twisted and his shirt untucked.

"It's okay," I said, reaching out a hand, but not across the desk. I didn't touch. Touch seemed dangerous.

"You're scaring me."

"Louisa. You tell him."

"It's just, well, the doctor said—"

She stopped. It was cruel, but she was lost now, her eyes afloat, in saltwater down to her chin. Ryan's face went pink—he was as fair as Lou, and more susceptible to emotional colouring—and his eyes found mine, pleading: *Throw me a line. What the fuck?*

"Remission," I said. The word was gentle; it landed softly in my mouth. "He didn't say for sure. He said almost."

The desk was gone somehow, his arms around us. The earth shifted and the newspaper's deadline loomed and the light angled slightly lower over the desks, the bent heads and the marked-up copy. We didn't notice. Our eyes were closed.

A half-hour later, Louisa and I sat in a booth at Lime Rickey's, on the second floor in the Eaton Centre. Huge, cheery, lime-green wedges of plastic looked down on us from the ceiling, and a mini jukebox sat on the Formica, next to the pepper and salt. The Super Chocolate Fudge Brownie Deluxe arrived. It was just like in the picture: a chocolate volcano in mid-eruption. We jabbed our sundae spoons in.

I smiled across the booth at Lou. She smiled back, ate a few spoonfuls, and then sat back as though it was hard work, eating. Whatever Dr. Q had said couldn't change the fact that her appetite had been decimated. The adrenalin was deserting me; I could feel it draining: down from the forehead, over the cheeks, through the neck. The table was still damp from being wiped clean, but I had to fight not to lay my head down upon it. I needed a word with Mr. Oncologist. What did he mean by *almost*, exactly? How much emphasis had he put on that word versus *remission*? Why say it at all if he wasn't sure?

We'd always been superstitious, Lou and I, in a non-committal, schoolgirl fashion. What I mean is, you make the forces work your way. Like how we used to buy the monthly horoscope scrolls at Shoppers Drug Mart, circle our lucky days and numbers, grab a calendar, and figure out how these coincided with our schedules: Was that a Day Two, when I had math class with Jason? Did that day fall on one of Lou's performances? When we read our tea leaves, we mainly hunted the cups for the shapes of letters that matched the initials of certain significant others. Once, Lou signed out a book on palm-reading. She said my lifeline was long and deeply etched. Hers was fine and frayed, but it had a double. We puzzled over that but refrained from seeking answers in the book. (Did we really want to know?) A double line matched a life in the theatre: alternate personalities. It meant she would start over one day, choose a new path.

We examined and re-examined my disturbing heartline, which split off halfway across my palm and petered out. Where was it going, my heart? Why did it seem to dissolve?

Quietly, we chewed, we swallowed, we looked around at the others in the restaurant. Something was wrong here. Something had been wrong from the moment we set foot in the school and opened our mouths. It was as if we'd taken the good news and spread it too thinly, like a person trying to love too many people at once.

With coffee and tea, tax and tip, the bill came to fourteen dollars. We paid it, put on our coats, and walked out into the stream of mall shoppers. We hugged. Lou turned south, to meet her mother at work and catch a subway home. I walked the other way.

Back in the kitchen, the grilled cheese was in the frying pan, dry and hard. The faint scent of toast clung to the room. I picked up the pan, walked over to the garbage can, flipped the lid, and dumped the sandwich in.

TWELVE

The Wolf

THE NEWSPAPERS AND RADIOS WERE ABUZZ WITH reports that Quebec premier Robert Bourassa had entered a hospital south of the border to begin an experimental treatment, not yet approved in Canada, for metastatic malignant melanoma. This treatment had so far greatly helped 40 percent of patients who'd received it.

This treatment was harsh, but promising.

This treatment was being offered to a famous politician, but not to my best friend.

"Because *he's* important," I said. Fuming. Ryan patted my shoulder, shook his head. It wasn't right.

The doctor had been right to be wary about using the word *remission*. Within a few short months, Lou's tumours had begun to grow again. I had known—of course I had known, that day we sat over our super deluxe brownies in the mall. Knowing wasn't the point. I was disappointed, frustrated, angry, crushed. When would someone figure this thing out? When could Lou just get back to normal? I missed what now seemed like our old, worry-free life.

And anyway, how could they—*they* as in whoever distributed second chances, whoever made these calls weighted in favour of those already favoured—be so sure Louisa wouldn't develop into a member of society as significant and influential as Bourassa? Or more so? She'd been high school valedictorian, after all. She'd roused our fellow students into protest. She'd hosted TV shows with flair and charisma. She acted, sang, wrote, directed, agitated, entertained, led—showed passion and promise. Shouldn't we pull out all the stops for her, too, just in case she was meant to become someone special?

Fuck that. Louisa was already someone special.

SHORTLY AFTER HER DISEASE PICKED UP STEAM AGAIN, Lou requested a leave of absence from school. She was missing too much class. She couldn't keep up. And, she told me, her mind just wasn't on her studies. She took more shifts at Eaton's and settled into a different kind of life.

We muddled through the rest of the year, my third and final year of journalism, and what would have been, had she stayed enrolled, Lou's second year in RTA. By now I'd been in a relationship with Ryan for more than a year, and Louisa had come around so completely that our early argument about him was a running joke between us.

I'd say, "Remember that time you told me to reject Ryan?"

"You're kidding! I said he'd be the best thing that ever happened to you."

"Uh-huh. You always know what's best for me."

Meanwhile, against all my private predictions, Louisa and Glen were still together, as "together" as two people can be when several large provinces are laid out between them. They couldn't let each other go, despite how impractical their situation was. Lou was still periodically plagued with doubt, but usually she was more focused on finding a cheaper long-distance package. I told myself to trust her instincts: they had to be stuck on Glen for a reason. Perhaps that reason was a good one after all.

I became used to the condo with its high ceilings and commanding view of Lake Ontario. In the centre of the living room, against a backdrop of tall windows, was the white chesterfield, still pristine, that Lou and I had been warned not to sit on back in grade nine. That was over now. The couch was eight years old, and we, technically, were adults. We could sit wherever we pleased. But I still felt uneasy going near it.

In springtime Ryan and I and the rest of our journalism cronies graduated, which seemed to underline the unfairness of Lou's situation. I quickly landed my first full-time job, as a reporter at a monthly local magazine. We talked about this with our usual excitement, as though Lou would get right back to her "real" life soon enough. When I stayed over at the condo, we'd lounge on the white couch—Lou would coax me to sit there with her—and stare out the window. We'd watch sitcoms. Occasionally we'd muster ourselves, gather our gear, and head to the pool on the seventh floor.

We'd tried the pool for the first time during winter. Halfway across its oblong, irregular shape, a glass partition descended from the ceiling to a foot above the water. You could paddle underneath, exiting the confines of the clean, quiet tower to find yourself not just beholding the downtown skyline but inhabiting it. We swam submerged, fishlike, making neither splash nor ripple, toward the far end. I closed my eyes against the chlorine, held my breath, and kicked. When I finally needed air I veered upward, cracking the surface. The cold hit me like a slap. I shrank down, resting my chin in the water's warmth. I saw Louisa standing nearby, the surface encircling her waist, steam rising around her. Water beaded her cheeks, her nose, her neck. I followed her gaze. *The Royal York* in red script stared back from the hotel's green copper roof. Behind it, the night gleamed in the gold-tinted glass of the bank towers, the very glass that had shone with promise the day we'd moved to the city nearly three years before. *Welcome*, I'd imagined those buildings murmuring, a chorus of welcomes for me and my friend, who had come here to do great things.

By summertime, Louisa seldom felt like going for a swim.

JUNE SANK INTO HUMIDITY. MOSQUITOS BUZZED OUR ankles as we strolled along the harbourfront one evening. Our lazy conversation turned to Vancouver. At first, I wasn't alarmed. We often discussed Vancouver: the far-off, mysterious, rain-drenched home of Lou's boyfriend. Hang on, though. This was different. This wasn't lazy chit-chat, not anymore. Lou was proposing—*what?*

She was going to move there, all the way across the country, to Vancouver. So she could be with Glen, of course.

No, no, no, bad idea. Trying to sound neutral, I asked what she would do out there. I didn't add to that, "other than follow Glen around."

"I'll get a job."

"What kind?"

"Maybe Eaton's will let me switch."

"Cosmetics."

"Yeah, why not? I like it. It pays okay. It doesn't tire me out too much."

"I think it's good that you got that job."

"You do?"

"Yeah, of course." I meant it. It wasn't super taxing. She didn't have to "take it home" with her. Her colleagues were nice. She felt busy and capable—she had a gift for making people feel like they looked good.

"I'm glad."

I had the feeling some misunderstanding had been cleared up. But I had never disapproved of the cosmetics job. Had I? Did she think I was disappointed that she'd left school? What choice did she have? Maybe she was secretly glad she'd left. Maybe her ambition was waning. Being happy at Eaton's would be a giant clue. But I didn't care. I just wanted her to be okay.

And I wanted her to stay.

"It rains all the time. You'll get depressed."

"I'm already depressed. My mom's requested a transfer too. She wants a fresh start."

"You're *both* moving?"

"If she gets the transfer, they'll even pay for the move."

This was for real. It wasn't just an idea. They'd go in September—two months away.

IN AUGUST, IN THE MIDST OF THEIR MOVING PREPARATIONS, Lou's treatment changed again. Now it was to be something called Interferon, an anti-viral drug used to fight tumours. Like the Interleukin, it was an immune-booster. That was all I understood, except that it seemed harsher in practice. During the treatment, Louisa would experience such violent chills that her mother, or a nurse, or I, would heap wool blanket after wool blanket on top of her. You couldn't speak to her then; you just sat with her through the torment. It began to feel like we were putting her through a series of trials, each more cruel than the last. If she survived all these "treatments," she would be allowed to go forth in the universe unencumbered. The gods would owe her.

One night we were in her mom's bedroom watching TV, the three of us all scrunched together on the queen-sized bed, when Lou started to cry. Her mother and I looked at each other. Where had this come from? Then her mother took her in her arms and said, "What is it? What's wrong?"

"I'm scared."

"There's nothing to be afraid of," her mother said.

"I can't help it. I'm scared all the time."

It wasn't fair. Some instinct was making her afraid, but it wasn't like a warning that would help her escape when the wolf showed up. If this predator came, she wouldn't get away. Maybe it was better to ignore the possibility of the wolf entirely. Or to just shrug and say, *Well, if it comes, it comes. What can I do?* But how does one learn to not bother with fear when fear is useless? I sat on the bed while Lou's mother held her and stroked her head and murmured in her ear. There might have been a time when I could have talked with Lou about the questions in my mind, when she might have gotten involved in trying to solve the problem of fear—what was the point of it, in a situation such as this?— but that time had passed. She was through analyzing and questioning. She was *feeling*: She was bowled over by it. This was why she'd left our co-op. This was why she needed her mother. Not for strategies or plans—our forte. Not even for understanding. For comfort.

The next morning, her mother already gone to work, I sat in the kitchen at the condo—there are so many kitchens in our history—the light streaming in from across the lake, eating a morning glory muffin from a batch Lou had baked the day before. Baking was a new thing she was trying.

"This is great. I'm impressed," I said, my mouth half full.

Lou stood by the counter, exhibiting no signs of last night's terrors, asking if there was anything else she could get me.

She's treating me like a guest, I thought. *I've turned into a guest.*

THE NIGHT BEFORE LOU AND HER MOTHER LEFT FOR Vancouver, I stayed with them in a hotel room downtown. Their belongings had already been shipped. They'd booked a suite. I got the pull-out couch, where I lay restless and wakeful all night, certain that, in the room next door, Louisa wasn't sleeping either. Nights had not improved for her; she often woke up with pain. As I tossed in the hotel blankets, I couldn't fathom how she managed. The night is a dark pit, seemingly bottomless, into which we go down alone. I thought about getting up and going to her in the next room, but I was so tired, and I had work early in the morning, and if she actually was sleeping, I didn't want to disturb her.

They had to be at the airport before 7 a.m. When we said goodbye, we were still half-asleep. It was better that way, we agreed. As I walked out of the hotel and up Yonge Street, it occurred to me that this move was all for the best: I would get used to not having her around before she was actually gone.

I caught my breath. I walked faster. I pushed my way north, trying not to think. Obviously, I could no longer trust myself to think.

Part Three

THIRTEEN

Long Distance

A SLEEPY-EYED PEACE HOVERED OVER REGENT PARK IN THE morning. I'd often think how the quiet spaces and grassy areas between buildings would have made sense on paper, but that no one foresaw how all those hidden nooks would be commandeered by people with every reason not to be seen. It was March, mucky and pungent. As warmer weather crept along the pathways between buildings, the people in Regent Park and the cops on the beat here would say, "Wait till summer. That's when all hell breaks loose." That's when the children are home from school and their playgrounds are ringed with dealers, and dealers' recruiters, and every time I saw a child on a swing or chasing a ball, I'd think to myself, *That's right, play, keep your eye on the ball, don't look at what else is around you.*

I tried not to look myself and, in that way, I wasn't much of a reporter. Rather, I was a one-sided reporter, looking instead for the people doing good, the stories that showed the real, everyday lives of ordinary people. I thought it was important to make known that most people in this neighbourhood, in this place that so many outsiders wrote off as violent and criminal, were simply going about their business, doing their best.

The magazine I worked for, the *T.O!*, was out today, and I looked forward to seeing it after the mad scramble to get it to press. I'd written on new tango and hip-hop classes for kids at the Cabbagetown Youth Centre. And I'd interviewed Nick Scountrianos from the Parliament Grill, who described what he called daily episodes of *Cops* on the street outside his restaurant. The assignment made me think of Ryan, who worked part-time as a security guard at Sears. Floorwalkers, they were called. We were still together. It'd been well over two years. It felt solid. But my mind had started wandering during his tales of shoplifter-catching exploits. I wasn't sure I liked the side of him that those stories revealed.

As I walked through the park, others made their way to streetcar stops and schoolyards, or got into cars and drove off deeper into the city. I thought about the people I couldn't see, the ones inside with nowhere to rush off to, like the elderly and housebound: kettles boiling and slices of bread dropping into toasters. I thought about Lou and Glen in Vancouver.

It wasn't yet 6 a.m. out west. Were they lying in bed together, the early light creeping over them both? Had she slept? I'd slept, and then awoke feeling guilty for not having thought much about how Lou was doing for a week or so. I had been too caught up in my deadline mania. I sometimes felt guilty for spending my days in Regent Park and then leaving to go home at night, to a street that felt airier and lighter, where gardens spilled over and the bricks and porches were all different colours. I was only dipping a toe into these tougher worlds, Louisa's and the Park's, then lifting it out and shaking it off.

Lou had been living with Glen since September. Her move out west had been a huge leap, a show of purpose and faith—the end of their emotional long-distance declarations, sometimes for, sometimes against a future together. At last, a decision. A home, even, which Glen had found before Louisa arrived, surprising her with a view of English Bay from their apartment. But neither the view nor finally feeling secure in this relationship had cured her. Glen had recently taken a leave from the communications program he'd transferred to at Simon Fraser University. They were both out of school now, only halfway to their degrees. Managing Louisa's cancer had become the central focus of their lives.

Over the phone, late at night—I was the one who had to accommodate the three-hour time difference now—I'd entertain Louisa with tales of life at the *T.O!*, where I was closing in on my fourth season as a reporter in the heart of the largest public housing project in the country. Our office was on the second floor of a high-rise, in what would have otherwise been two apartment units. We had official documents, fat reports, notes and old newspapers strewn and heaped on our desks and on the floor. On a filing cabinet in the corner teetered Tupperware containers filled with the mutating remains of uneaten lunches. Our computers were framed in a heavy-duty, yellowing plastic; they were pre-Windows, and our keyboards were equipped with function-key menus on loose strips of paper (F7 to print). Our desks faced each other in U formation; I sat along one arm and spent a good deal of time trying not to watch my colleagues and good friends, Adam and Spence, hurl insults—and sometimes objects—at one another across the no-man's land in the centre of the room.

"Spence, Spence, you can't be serious" was one of Adam's favourite lines.

From Spence, not infrequently: "Why do you torment me, man? Why? I'm just trying to do my work here. I'm just trying to be a good person."

Every cutting jibe was really an attempt to entertain its victim. It required a good deal more physical effort than the friendship I enjoyed with Lou: sometimes there was actual wrestling. But I sensed a similar current running beneath all that fuss.

Now and then from the office next door would emit a strangled plea for calm from our editor, Joseph, who claimed his heritage to be either—and he would deeply despise me for forgetting which—Greek or Macedonian, speaking often and with relish of the historic animosity between the two ethnicities. He swore by bananas, onions, and garlic—"Miracle foods!" he'd call them, emphatically pointing a long finger at the ceiling. He'd stand in the doorway, running a hand through his unkempt hair and groaning. "Gentlemen. A little decorum, please!" But he only did this out of duty. He couldn't keep from smiling, even as he raised his voice.

I told Lou that Joseph had decided to add an astrology feature to the magazine. He happened to know a "real" astrologer, whose work, he assured us, was nothing like the bumph you saw in the newspaper. Adam was furious. "Serious journalism," he'd grumble, as we strolled to the local convenience store to buy Styrofoam cups of acrid coffee. "That's what we're here for. These people don't need horoscopes!"

Lou interrupted me. "He's showing off," she said. "He's hot for you." This was an old conversation, going all the way back to first year, when, after I'd taken a tumble skating on Lake Devo and gotten a hairline fracture in my elbow, Adam had given me a music box for my birthday, with a fallen figure skater atop it. A joke, but a rather extravagant one. I chose to ignore this, but Lou wouldn't let me.

"That's quite the present."

"He's just teasing me."

"Exactly."

Adam had a serious girlfriend. They'd met at one of the local community meetings he was covering for the *T.O!* Lou knew all about her, and how smitten Adam was. But I let her romanticize. Yeah, yeah, he was hot for me. Sure. Her insistence on this point was familiar. It was like old times.

SINCE WE WEREN'T ON DEADLINE ANYMORE, I GOT OFF work at five, like a normal person. I caught the streetcar, rode it swaying and screeching away from the park's brown brick townhouses and low-rise apartment blocks. As we trundled over the valley, I thought about Lou. It had been too long—never did Louisa and I go more than a week without talking. I felt myself willing the streetcar to pick up the pace, which only made its progress, ordinarily far from swift, feel that much slower.

Broadview Avenue was lined with rundown houses, the porches of which were sometimes shaded by bamboo blinds. I always noticed at least one old chrome-legged chair, its vinyl seat partly disemboweled, but not necessarily at the same house, on the same porch. The streetcar picked up a load of passengers. We passed the squat Riverdale library, the thick-walled Don Jail, and came to Riverdale Park, where that morning I'd seen a few angular, elderly Chinese men doing tai chi under a tree.

The last time I'd called Lou, I'd tried to stop Glen from automatically passing her the phone. "Wait! Are you sure she feels like talking?"

It was midnight in Toronto. I was pacing my bedroom with the phone nestled between my ear and my shoulder. He'd just told me she'd hardly slept for days because of the pain in her back. "Don't worry." His voice low, gentle. "She'll talk to you."

I spoke quietly too. Our old friend Nicky, now my roommate, was asleep in the room next door. "Maybe she doesn't want to."

"No. If it's you, I don't have to ask. You're in the inner circle."

"You mean you're screening her calls?"

"Yeah. Sometimes it's too much for her. Especially since the call from Sarah."

"Sarah?"

"She can tell you about it. Here."

Then Lou was in my ear saying, "Oh Anita, it was awful."

"What happened?"

Sarah was an old friend from high school, tall and sporty and friendly. She'd grown up in a big house in north Burlington with a heap of younger sisters. The family spent their weekends at a chalet on Blue Mountain. Sarah had taken Lou and me there once. It was nothing like the little cottages my family rented, or the tents Lou, her brothers, her dad, and stepmom piled into when they camped in Killbear Provincial Park. Sarah's family chalet was built out of gleaming pine logs. It sat high on a hill with a peaked roof and vast windows. The whole family skied and rock-climbed. This gave Sarah a branch of practical knowledge that neither Lou nor I had: what to wear in certain conditions, how to be safe in others. She had muscles and the nerve to go with them. She was a doer in a way that made me notice I moved through the world behind a veil of hesitation, assessing whether this or that action would be wise.

At the chalet, we slept in a loft that looked over the living room. I could have happily stayed up there all weekend, dangling my legs through the railings, taking in the crisp, wintry view. But Sarah dressed us in snow pants and set us up on the bunny hill while she went to race down the real slopes. She checked on us, encouraged us, and finally lured us higher. After an exhilarating ride up on a T-bar, Lou and I dropped awkwardly to the ground and stood side by side taking in the steep, white, icy slope. We looked at each other, nodded, and slid down on our bums.

We'd lost touch with Sarah. But she'd heard that Lou wasn't well and had called her.

"It was nice to talk to her," said Lou. "But then she said she wanted to come visit."

"Oh."

"I freaked out. I can't do it. I don't have the energy."

"Sarah wouldn't expect anything."

"I know. But she's not—I'd have to act like I was okay."

"You wouldn't."

"It's too much pressure. I can't explain it. But it gets worse. I got off the phone and started crying and saying to Glen, I don't want her to come. But I hadn't hung up properly. She was still there."

"Oh Louisa."

"I know. She called back and she said she was really sorry, she didn't want to upset me, she just wanted to help. And I had to tell her not to come."

"She'll understand. She's smart. She'll get it."

"I hope so."

I hoped so too. In our lives, some people are an automatic comfort. Some you have to gear up for. Lou might have been thinking about how much she'd changed since that goofy ride down Blue Mountain, and how she didn't want to see that register on Sarah's face when they first locked eyes. And how much there would be to explain from the intervening years. And maybe even that she didn't want to know about Sarah's life, and how wonderfully it was probably going, or at least how illness-free it was.

There was more to it though. I didn't grasp it then—I couldn't—but Lou was growing ruthless. Some part of her was willing her to pare down, to cut away, like when you clean out your closets before you move, only this cull was going be far more painful than giving away some old sweaters and shoes.

I hopped off the streetcar and walked the long block to where Nicky and I lived in a cozy basement apartment below a journalist couple with a toddler whose thumps on the floor over our heads had become background noise. I'd call Lou tonight, I thought. I'd wait till ten or so, when it would be seven in Vancouver. But when I unlocked the door the phone was ringing. I answered it to find Glen on the other end.

"Hey! I was going to call you guys later tonight." And why are *you* calling, instead of Louisa, I was about to ask, suddenly worried.

But Glen said, "Louisa's here. She wants to talk to you."

"Hi."

"Hi."

She said something in a whisper. I whispered back. "What was that?"

"I almost died today."

I sat. She spoke. I strained to hear.

She'd been to Toronto for a visit in January. She'd sat beside me on the couch. It'd been dark in the apartment, bear-den-like, with snow heaped against the small, high window that rested at ground level. I'd had the Yellow Pages open in my lap. We were flipping through, searching for a new place to try for supper. I was acting festive: It was my birthday; I was twenty-two. But when I'd opened the door to Louisa an hour earlier, I'd nearly gasped. She looked translucent, lit from within. Her cheekbones, once masked beneath the roundness of her face, were delicate sculptures. Her eyes floated above them like planets on a mobile.

She'd put her hand on mine, to stop me from flipping through the phone book.

"It's come back, you know. I can't do it anymore."

I raised my eyebrows in question.

"Swallow pills," she clarified.

"You're kidding? You have to do the juice thing again?" I had a vision of us in the kitchen, crushing a birth control pill between spoons. Ages ago, another world. *Louisa, Louisa*, I thought. *When are you going to stop being so dramatic?*

But she wasn't being dramatic. The pill-swallowing thing, she told me, wasn't exactly the same problem as before.

"How so?"

"I think I have a lump in my throat."

"You don't mean, like, a frog."

"I mean a lump."

We'd never gotten used to the word *tumour*. Or just preferred to avoid it.

Apparently, though, there hadn't been just one lump in her throat, but two. They'd been growing toward each other, unbeknownst to anyone, under the noses of all the medical people following Lou so closely—and had finally begun to cut off her airway. She couldn't breathe. That was how she'd nearly died. Now, in that voice I could barely hear, which seemed almost entirely devoid of Louisa herself, just puffs of air shaped like words, she explained that they'd shrunk the lumps with radiation. Emergency radiation. For now.

She had to pause. Her breathing was shallow and rasping. This was it, I thought. I never expected it would happen this way. Tumours in her throat!

But I didn't know what I'd expected.

She was saying, so softly I could barely catch the words, "You should come visit. Can you come?"

I could.

FOURTEEN

This Too Shall Pass

AT FIRST, RYAN SUGGESTED I GO ON MY OWN.

"I'd miss my mother's birthday." He drew his finger around the rim of the sweaty pint glass. We were at the Fox and Firkin. "I can't go on vacation and miss her birthday."

"This isn't a fucking vacation."

He said okay, he would come. I bought plane tickets—luckily, I had enough saved for both of us. Joseph let me book several days off between the next two issues. Adam and Spence promised to pick up the slack. The flights were in April, nearly a month away. I called Lou to tell her the plan.

"Great!"

"Are you sure?"

"Don't worry. I'm not going to die in the next few weeks."

I took the phone away from my ear and looked into the dark speaker holes. I couldn't believe we were talking this way. I didn't like it, this supernatural sense. She was in a different realm already, leaning away from us.

I'D ONLY EVER TRAVELLED BY PLANE AS AN INFANT; THIS was, in effect, my first experience of flying. As the vast jet raced down a runway at Pearson International Airport in Toronto, tipped its nose and began to smoothly rise, I felt an upswing of certainty, a sensation I can barely remember except to say that yes, once, I possessed it. Or it possessed me. There was no doubt. Of course we had to visit Lou. I was still winning the argument with Ryan, though it was long over. That buoyant feeling, that wonderful certainty, held for several hours, until the plane began its descent.

The Vancouver airport, like so much of the city, butts up against a sheltered arm of the Pacific Ocean. Some of its runways point seaward. As we flew lower and lower, I saw, rising to meet us, not a comforting yellow-striped tarmac, but steely grey water. I gripped Ryan's hand and stared into the rippling waves: thousands of little hatches opening up, then folding back into the depths. Just when I began to imagine the cold waves licking the belly of the plane, the runway was beneath us, the wheels touching down.

I thought I might chastise Lou and Glen. No, "Hey, by the way, if it looks like you're landing right smack in the ocean, don't sweat it. Totally normal." I was also excited: Here we were, in Vancouver! All the way across the country! Lou had been trying to lure me out here for months, raving about mountains and views and all the places we'd go. But, as Ryan and I left the arrivals gate and pushed our way through the crowd around the baggage carousels, I saw her.

She was standing behind a railing in frayed jeans. She wore her hair in a bob, as she had when I'd seen her three months before. But her face was misshapen and swollen. It was like looking through a mask to see her own much smaller face, way down, far beneath the swelling. Ryan and I wove through a throng of people. Then I was near enough: I tapped her on the shoulder. She turned.

"Hey." She smiled and the real Lou flashed through. I stepped forward to hug her.

She stiffened. "Careful."

I lightly circled my arms around her shoulders, trying not to notice whether my hands brushed over any tumours. I stepped back and she took me in.

"Your hair!"

"I know. I got it cut off."

"Wow. You look so sophisticated."

"It was liberating," I said, showing off my neck.

I wondered how she felt knowing I'd just marched effortlessly through the airport, my health and strength intact. But I was tired and rumpled from the flight, and, upon seeing her, even more rattled than when she'd told me a few weeks earlier that she'd literally stopped breathing. I would never have grouped myself among those who rush off to the salon after every fight with a boyfriend, every disappointment at work. Yet here I was, in the face of Louisa's latest disaster, transformed.

Before we'd left Toronto, Lou had told me that the scar tissue from the radiation on her throat might eventually cause as much of a problem as the lumps themselves. Someday soon—"soon" being an indeterminate time frame—she might simply stop breathing. The air would have no way in. The kicker was, now that it had almost happened, she wasn't afraid to die.

"It wasn't scary," she'd said on the phone. "It was really peaceful."

I was glad she wasn't scared, truly. But as she stood so serenely by the circling suitcases, exuding her new willingness to "go" gracefully, I panicked. Hurrah for grace. Fuck grace. I had to stop myself from grabbing her by the arm and hightailing it out of there. No, no! She isn't willing. She is afraid. You've got it all wrong.

AT THE APARTMENT IN TORONTO BACK IN JANUARY, after Lou had told me about the lump in her throat, I remembered the fat phone book in my lap. I couldn't bring myself to move it. Lou straightened her back and said something about elephants in the living room, how she needed to be able to talk about this stuff, and I said okay, not knowing or wanting to know what I was agreeing to. Then it happened.

Her funeral, she instructed, should not be a depressing affair, because she hadn't had a depressing life. It had been good and full, and she did not feel cheated. So there. No black. Spring flowers, she was saying. Tulips. Daisies. And that nice hymn about the sea and the sky. I knew the one she meant. And I'd like you to write something for me. She slipped it in, somewhere around the tulips and the hymn. You don't have to read it yourself, if you don't think you can, but would you write it?

"Of course. Of course I'll read it myself."

"Well, you don't know, you might not—"

"I will."

I asked no questions. I was too intent on making sure she understood I was unfazed. That was my job: to accept what she was handing me—which was so much less than what she'd been handed—without question. Hold steady as the wave engulfs the boat.

As I was so busy maintaining balance, I didn't learn a thing. For example: What would she like me to say? Or not say? Why me? Or better yet: Why were we discussing this at all? How could it possibly be necessary?

I finally set the phone book aside and got up. "I have to pee."

I sat on the toilet in the cramped bathroom Nicky and I did our best to keep clean and dry. I'd known Nicky nearly as long as I'd known Lou. She'd gone to high school with us and was now studying social work at Ryerson. It had taken some doing to convince her to move in with me. We were at a Bay Street coffee shop around the corner from her apartment, which was going to get too expensive in the fall. I was losing the room I'd rented for the summer at Esme's place—her regular room-mate would be back for the fall term. Fate, I proposed. Nicky dipped a spoon in her café au lait. She'd recently added some coppery red to her thin, fair hair. It glistened in the café light.

"I don't want to lose you as a friend."

"Everyone said that would happen to me and Lou. But we managed."

"That's different."

I frowned. It was, and it wasn't. Nicky understood how close Louisa and I were. But I didn't think being so close was the reason we'd done okay. Indeed, that had made moving in together more dangerous. I fixed her with my steely, don't-argue-with-me look. Louisa was not suscepti-ble to this look, but Nicky might be.

"My gut tells me this will be good," I said. "We should trust my gut. It usually works."

The apartment we found was one of those basements about which you say, "It doesn't *feel* like a basement." Entering, which you did from the back door off a little patio, descending a narrow staircase and turning past the washer and dryer, was like walking into a modest sanctuary: it was more enclave than cave. And it stayed blessedly cool on hot days.

In the old days in quiet Burlington, Nicky and I had a game we played when we ran into one another in the hallways of our high school: we would make eye contact, chant "Flowers, flowers, they grow!" and then bow our heads and snap our fingers really fast. This was our tribute to the Beats, of whom, truth be told, we knew precious little. We did this the day we moved in, standing next to the stool, heads bowed. I imagined Louisa sauntering in and rolling her eyes, as she had always done whenever she'd witnessed this display. I enjoyed her reaction to this little ritual, because I was usually the one rolling my eyes at her.

Sometimes we'd spot a fat centipede, a blurred grey smudge darting across the bathroom floor. None today. Instead, a vision of Louisa in another bathroom, a hospital bathroom, flashed to mind. The scene was from the day she and her parents had their first conference with Dr. Q, the day the C-word was officially ushered into use. I hadn't been there, but I could see her in the stall as she'd described herself in that moment, smacking her hand against the metal door until she had no choice but to cry.

That was three and a half years ago. I gripped the sides of the toilet seat with both hands, feeling the cool porcelain against my palms. So much had happened since then: treatments, surgeries, and sickness; boyfriends, parties, jobs, exams; bedrooms, kitchens, pools; movies and wars. And good news that never seemed to last. I was staring, as I often did, at the illustrated poster Nicky and I had thumbtacked to the door. We'd picked it up for free at a publisher's booth at Word on the Street that fall. That was the day Nicky spotted Margaret Atwood not more than a few feet away, smaller in stature than we ever would have expected, her nose angular and sharp, her hair springing out in all directions. Seeing her was stirring: like a promise that the ideas and people alive in your mind might leap into reality at any time.

The poster contained four panels showing a squat figure in a white gown, his back to the viewer and his hands clasped behind him, watching a scene unfold before him. First, a vast ship with a face in every portal. Then a trolley full of passengers. Third, a parade, complete with drummer, clown, and unicyclist. Fourth, nothing at all: a blank vista. Beneath each illustration was the proverb, "This too shall pass." I was fond of the man in the poster, his attention and his patience. Events moved and shifted before him, but he, with his mysterious, unseen face, held fast. He never turned away. Everything, he wanted me to understand, was temporary: celebration, journeys, joy, bleak uncertainty. Attention must be paid. Even nothingness itself, though it might roll down the street right before our eyes, would keep on moving and disappear. Something would follow. The space would fill in.

I stood up, suddenly hungry. It was my birthday, and Louisa was here. I reached out, turned the chrome knob, and passed right by the man on the poster to where she was waiting.

BY THE TIME RYAN AND I ARRIVED IN VANCOUVER, THREE months later, the promise I'd made to Louisa, to be the one to speak for her—after, when, if—had settled into me so naturally that I mostly didn't think of it. It wasn't that I'd set the promise aside or forgotten it. We adjust, that's all. We get on with things. And we quietly hope some of the adjustments we've made will prove unnecessary—that things will change, and revert to an old, familiar reality.

Actually, though, being in Louisa's presence made that past reality seem more lost to us than ever. Walking to the car from the arrivals lounge, we moved slowly, a light drizzle spraying our faces and coats. I'd let my pace pick up without realizing it, so I had to keep pausing and circling back, steering Ryan with me.

Behind us, Glen stepped cautiously along beside Lou, his thick dark hair as airy and blow-dried as ever. A smile had taken over his face, broad and helpless. "I can't believe you guys are here," he said. "I'm sorry about the rain. It was sunny yesterday, honest." His voice was *like* the rain, low and flowing.

Louisa laughed. "Glen's been worried about the weather all week."

I remembered how disarming he was, how warm, all the stuff that had hooked Lou right off. "It's not like we had any illusions," I said.

"It's rotten luck," said Glen. He shook his head. "Typical."

Louisa stopped moving. Glen's hand was on her elbow, flash. "What's up?"

"I just need to rest for a minute."

Glen looked up at Ryan and me. "This is incredible, you know. Last week she couldn't even get out of bed." His happiness over Louisa's successful inching forward lit his cheeks.

Lou saw my questioning look. "It's true. I lost a lot of muscle in the hospital."

Muscle? She'd lost muscle? There was always some extra terrible detail, something I hadn't kept on top of. I fell back, so Glen and I held her between us in a kind of force field as we walked on. I nudged her. "I knew it would rain. We'll be drenched all week."

"Don't tease him too much," she said, quietly. "He wants you guys to like it here."

Finally, not that deep into the parking lot, but what seemed a long, long way from the luggage carousels, we dumped our bags in the back of Glen's Tercel. I crawled in behind the passenger seat. Ryan got in on the other side. Our eyes met overtop a giant makeup bag with a gaudy floral print, sort of "Hawaiian Skirt Meets Fort Lauderdale Dollar Store." I sent Ryan a thought: *I'm glad you're here.* He sent one back: *I'm glad I came.*

"What's in the ugly bag?"

"Open it," Lou said.

I unzipped the flap, expecting a jumble of lipstick, compacts, and mascara. Inside was a cavalcade of small brown pill bottles. "Oh my God. You take them everywhere?"

"I have to. I need to take something like every two hours."

"Okay. But why do you keep them in such an ugly bag?" I hoped this would make her laugh. It didn't.

"It's the biggest bag I have."

"I'll buy you a new one while I'm here." I couldn't stop.

"I don't think it's ugly."

"Sure you do. I know you do."

But then she and Glen realized she was late taking something, maybe the steroid—the pill that caused the swelling in her face, wrists, and ankles. I passed the bag forward. Glen started rummaging. "I'm always forgetting something," Lou said, frustration rising.

"It's okay," said Glen softly. "You can take it now."

"You're right. It's no big deal."

In that exchange was a great, indecipherable unsaid— some current running between them through which they passed understandings back and forth. I stopped listening; it felt like eavesdropping.

I busied myself checking out the to-do list for our trip, which Lou had handed me in the airport. We had just ten days before Ryan and I flew back home, two of which Lou would spend at the B.C. Cancer Agency getting her next dose of chemo. In that time, as per her list, we were to visit Stanley Park, Granville Island, Grouse Mountain, UBC, North Van, Capilano, Victoria, Whistler, Shannon Falls, Glen's "homeland" of Langley, and a place called Hell's Gate that, despite its name, was apparently the most beautiful place Lou had ever seen.

"God, Lou," I said—after, with difficulty, she'd swallowed her medication. "We can just hang out."

"I've been waiting to show you these places."

"I didn't come out here to be entertained." I said this in this way I have, which tells you I'm offended for being underestimated.

"I can sit at home or I can sit in the car," she said. "It hurts to lie down. I might as well sit in the car."

I had a flash of awareness, a glint of something approaching grace. She needed to bring her idea of this visit to life. Make it real. This wasn't about me.

After a tour through town in the reliable old Tercel, including a stop at a totem pole in Stanley Park, we steered into the parking garage below their apartment building, not far from the Burrard Street bridge. Their block was tree-lined, shady, and packed with buildings that had been there long enough to look cozy and worn-in, like the brick-and-concrete equivalent of old sweaters. In the garage, there were two steps leading to the elevators. Lou paused before them and gripped Glen's shoulder. Her face tight with concentration, she lifted one leg, then another, up the first step. She stopped to breathe, then climbed the second. We all shuffled into the elevator, let the doors close, and began to rise.

WHEN GLEN HAD MOVED BACK TO B.C. AFTER FIRST YEAR, I'd hoped his importance to Lou would wane in proportion to his distance. But once Louisa and Glen were actually living together in their apartment-with-a-view, I'd begun to coach myself to think of him differently. Not as the guy who'd been Louisa's tortuous emotional see-saw, but as the guy who gave her that thoughtful gift the first Christmas they were together: her own personal teapot. Not as the guy who turned up his nose at Toronto, but as the guy who bowed his head apologetically and said, "Forget it," after telling a joke. Not as the source of Lou's gargantuan long-distance bill but as a guy who liked hanging out with his older sisters and who never complained about his complicated mother. I thought of his dark hair flopping over his eyes and what that did to Lou. His sharp (yet modest) intellect; his ability to see through the bullshit in the news without, as I often did, taking it personally; his basic kindness. I couldn't help but think of Lou's oblique allusions to their sex life, which sounded wonderful in ways I couldn't comprehend—what did she mean she "lost all inhibition"? Louisa the Virgo, Louisa the Perfectionist, Louisa who'd once written to herself, "Stop watching yourself and just live"? *That* Louisa, uninhibited? Some alchemy had to factor in, a magic I had yet to experience in my own stilted explorations. Lou's instincts had led her to Glen. Stuck her, actually. And he'd finally come around to a decision that, though it took her away from me, made her happy. He was onside. We were allies now.

The end of doubt and uncertainty was a relief, even to me. But their relationship at that time should have been the least of my worries. On September 10, 1993, shortly after arriving in Vancouver, Louisa met with a doctor at the B.C. Cancer Agency, the woman who would become her new oncologist. The specialist's resident took an account of Louisa's medical history, all the way back to the beginning, noting that after her first surgery at age twelve, she was free of disease until April 1990, when she had a mass removed from under her arm (that lump she'd found while we were still in high school). The following year's tumour in the same arm was noted, as was a lesion later removed from her groin, then the lumps that began to appear along her collarbone, arms, and midriff while she was on levamisole, which hadn't seemed like such an obvious failure during the months she was on it. The resident taking notes painstakingly described the multiple tumours now scattered over Lou's trunk, front and back, as well as her neck, groin, and armpits. I don't think Lou or I, or Glen, perhaps not even her parents, quite realized what the oncologist would have instantly understood while studying that report: things had been steadily getting worse for years. It was as though our instinctive adjustment to each setback shielded us from the harsh reality behind it.

I had been getting updates from Lou herself, during lengthy phone calls between Vancouver and Toronto. The Interferon was giving her headaches and nausea. Some of her tumours had grown inflamed. They itched and leaked puss. Did this mean the treatment was vigorously attacking them, or that they were simply turning into open sores? We speculated about this on the phone. The new doctor suspected infection and prescribed an antibiotic: 500 mg of Cloxacillin four times per day. Yet more drugs. She also recommended that Louisa sustain as high a dose of Interferon as she could stand, and Lou was game. She wanted to pummel this disease.

Lou, who'd been described in her newly composed medical history as "an unfortunate, young, very pleasant lady with metastatic melanoma," was to return to the doctor two weeks later, but she called sooner to complain of new oozing from one of the tumours on her chest. She was put on more antibiotics and saw the doctor again a few days later. This was late September, a glorious time of year back in Toronto, when the heat of summer had dissipated, leaving air that was fresh and cool. I'm not sure Lou was noticing the weather in Vancouver much: she worriedly told her new oncologist she was experiencing shortness of breath, palpitations, and dizziness. One of the tumours measured two weeks before had slightly shrunk, but an ultrasound revealed a 3 by 3.5 cm mass under the abdominal wall that had not been there at the time of her last ultrasound, three months earlier, back in Toronto. The doctors had no idea whether this had turned up before or after she'd started on Interferon, so close monitoring, including ultrasounds every four to six weeks, were planned.

The last line of Lou's medical history, as recorded by the doctor's resident, read, "It is worth mentioning that Louisa does not know exactly the dose of Interferon she is taking right now." Maybe this observation ought to be alarming, but when I revisit my copy of this deeply distressing document, which her family kindly shared with me—am I still hoping for some obscure clue to emerge, a way out that we missed?—reading it makes me smile. It shows a bit of Louisa-style spunk: I'll take this drug, I'll do as I'm told, but I won't spend my whole life thinking about it.

That's how I choose to read it, anyway. She wasn't feeling spunky, not at all. Here is a journal entry from that time, one of the few she wrote:

Sept. 23/93

I know I need help. I'm starting to get a kind of defeatist attitude. I mean I feel quite happy a lot of the time and quite ecstatic some of the time. Glen is wonderful—he's so loving and supportive and he'll do anything for me. But then I feel guilty because I should be fighting like crazy for my life with him. If I could get better it would be everything. I have too much to live for. But sometimes the disease just seems so big—it's all I can see. The lady who did my ultrasound at the Cancer Agency said she had been diagnosed with cervical cancer. She seemed so confident that I could beat this. It was weird cause I'm not used to people talking so positively—well at least people who don't have to. Like Glen and Mom—they have to believe I'm not going to die. But this lady, she has no stakes in my life, and she talked like she knew, and I've been thinking about it ever since. She believed in me—with no strings—with nothing to gain or lose. I keep hearing her voice very matter-of-factly saying, "I mean, you're bigger than this thing." And then she went on talking about how I feel unsure now but it's because I'm in the middle of my crisis but when, and again she said this very matter-of-factly, "but when your remission comes and you stop being scared all the time, you'll figure it out."

Anyway, I guess her attitude made me realize how far off mine is. My mind isn't where it should be. Fear is very prevalent. I don't know if I fear more now because I see how great my life is with Glen—and I fear losing that. Or because maybe I'm just starting to give up. But I don't want to give up. I want to fight because I have everything to live for. She told me I had to "get stubborn with it."

I have to find the strength—I need help.

L

She got her transfer and started work at the downtown Eaton's—that helped. She started making new friends there, which also helped. But the cancer agency documents on Lou's checkups throughout that autumn consistently report "progression of disease" and "probable progression of disease" and "probable advancing of disease on Interferon." She was raised from 2 megaunits of Interferon per day to 3, though even at the low dose the Interferon had made her anemic, then to 5, and then finally, in late November, to 7 and "possibly to 10 megaunits if this is well tolerated." She started taking Tylenol 3 for pain and was sent for consultation on radiation treatment. I didn't understand it at the time, but this was purely palliative. The radiologist determined that several of her tumours would respond positively to this, including one on her scalp that worried her for "cosmetic" reasons. "She is a cosmetician," the document reads, "and she is afraid that this will become obvious and make it difficult for her to continue working. Her work is clearly an important part of her life."

It's hard not to read incredulity between the lines. Did the doctors find it surprising that this young cancer patient should care about having a job? On October 29, it is noted that, "Following the visit last week Miss Prose became depressed that the lesions did not seem to be getting smaller." Further down the same page the following observation appears: "On examination at the present time, Miss Prose overall appears slightly pale but in excellent health."

I stop on this line. I read it again. Does it really say "excellent"? It does. I imagine this means her pulse is strong, her blood pressure sound, her organs all doing their thing. Still, there must be something missing, like, say, the phrase "under the circumstances." For a girl with a body addled with tumours, some of them "weeping yellow material"; for a girl with a high white cell count and low iron; for a girl injecting herself with interferons every morning; for a girl who could get through the day only with the help of heavy-duty painkillers; indeed, Miss Prose was in excellent health.

Around this time Lou began keeping an audio journal on a cassette tape. It seemed easier than writing things down, and also allowed her to use some of the tech skills she'd picked up at Ryerson. She'd do a sound check at the start of each entry, grunting in frustration if the dials weren't co-operating. I have a copy kindly dubbed for me by Glen on a dual-cassette player. Of all the things I keep, this tape is the most precious to me, for it contains her voice. It's not exactly her voice as I would like to remember it. It's shakier, more faint, less hearty. But it's still Lou's slightly nasal pitch, and when I hear it I can see her whole face behind it: the compact mouth forming the words, the nostrils flaring when she's particularly passionate, the high forehead and light freckle pattern over her cheeks. I see her deep-red hair tucked behind her ear, her long pale fingers gesturing to her imaginary audience.

That is not to say I *enjoy* listening to this tape. The things Louisa says are not, as I remember Ronald Regan pronouncing in a speech after the 1986 space shuttle disaster, "for the faint of heart." He was such a tough-guy president, excluding "the faint of heart" from working boldly toward a different kind of future. I think for many of us, it's the past, not the future, that's the truly frightening place to go.

Testing out my volume, move that up a little bit. Hello? Okay. I'm recording this, this is the day back from my trip, I just got up about an hour ago. And, um [her voice breaks], I'm in a lot of pain [breaks again]. I'm in a lot of pain a lot of the time. And um, once the drugs kick in it's fine, but until the drugs kick in, it's a terrible feeling. Pain, in my stomach, and achiness and pains through my neck, down my arms, um, and basically I have to get up in the morning, and you know, most people plan, they get up in time to have a shower, and to have some breakfast and get ready to go to work. But I have to get up in time to make sure that my painkillers are working in time for me to start to get ready for me to go to work. And this is one of those mornings. It's a definite downside of the whole thing. Um, so, basically, I'm on three different types of painkillers, and one of them is a stream of morphine, so it makes me feel very drugged. So, I try not to take that during the day too much. But I definitely take it at night, I don't know, it seems that at night the pain is the worst. You lie there alone and nothing will make it go away. So, I tend to over-drug myself at night, so I can sleep. But as soon as the painkillers start to work, everything's okay. And I just try and lead my day as normal as possible, and stay on top of the pain. The doctor said it's easier to keep the pain away than chase it away once it's there. So I just keep taking them, every four to six hours, two or three pills. And, for the most part it keeps it away. [She laughs] A part of medical science that I'm very grateful for, obviously.

It was in the midst of all this that Glen requested a leave of absence and stopped going to school. He'd begun to drive Lou to her medical appointments, and that alone was a part-time job. I think, also—though he may not have acknowledged it, even to himself—that he feared his time with her would be short, and he wanted to be fully with her, not leading a parallel existence, rushing off to classes and holing up to write papers. I was grateful to him. I don't know if I could have done the same, or whether I'd even have understood the need. It may have been more than love that drove Louisa across the continent. Was there, in her, a driving instinct? An understanding of where and from whom she'd find the day-to-day support she'd come to need?

It's possible that, because Glen was with her every day, he got it better than I did. Maybe she confided in him more. He certainly saw more. Did I even realize she was fighting for her life? Maybe, yes. Sometimes. I remember once crying softly on the phone—she may not have known I was crying—as I told her, "But you're supposed to know my kids."

I was lying on my bed, staring at the ceiling.

"I know," she whispered in my ear. I could almost imagine we were back on one of the narrow beds in our student co-op, side by side late at night, talking through our problems.

"Our kids are supposed to get to know each other and hear stories about all the trouble we got into." What trouble? I thought, even as the words were forming. We'd been good girls. For the most part.

Louisa laughed softly. "Remember the time Nicky vacuumed up my puke?"

It was the only time I remember Lou having too much to drink. Nicky had spoken of the episode—even immediately afterward—matter-of-factly, as though she were vacuuming up puke all the time, as though the vacuum were the standard, obvious approach to vomit in inconvenient places. "Remember when everyone started *calling* me Puke?"

"That was hilarious."

"It's not like I was the only person who ever got sick."

"They just didn't expect it of you."

"I don't see why not."

Now, when I have the medical reports in my hands, when I slide Lou's journal into the machine and hit Play, I remember this conversation. I knew, I tell myself. There's no reason why these documents should shock me. Still, reading and listening can make me feel like I did when I was a kid and my brother, when we fought, would grip my wrist in both hands and turn the skin in opposite directions. Every hard, recorded fact, every hesitation or strain in Lou's voice, is a new twist. The skin pulls tighter. It stings and then it burns and then *Enough!*: I click Stop, or stuff the pages into the envelope till next time.

LOU AND GLEN WERE THE FIRST COUPLE WE KNEW TO move in together, and I noted on our first walk-through how their apartment was marked by them both. The yellow bedspread: Lou. The cheesy Elvis clock with the swinging hips: Glen. The giant spidery fern in the living room: Lou. The black bookcases in the living room: Glen. The clear division between her books and his: Lou. (She didn't want her copy of, say, *The Outsiders*, next to some textbook on communications theory.) The karaoke machine: Glen.

"You have one of these?" I asked. Ryan picked up the microphone.

"It's like when they sing 'Surrey with the Fringe on Top' in *When Harry Met Sally*."

"Ryan will sing for us."

"Oh no he won't."

There was a reclining white plastic lawn chair, complete with padding, in the living room, that looked utterly out of place beside the dark bookshelves and futon couch with its black cover. "Do you use that on the balcony?"

Lou shook her head. "Sometimes I spend half the night there. I sleep there."

"There?" It did not look comfortable.

"It works for my back."

"Your back hurts that badly?"

She smiled weakly and replied, "Everything hurts."

FIFTEEN

California Dreaming

THE ELVIS CLOCK ON THE WALL SWUNG ITS HIPS. IT WAS 5 a.m., still dark. Ryan was softly snoring beside me. I swallowed, wishing I could pretend away the unmistakable burning sensation in my throat. The bedroom door was ajar, and Louisa's breaths slipped through and floated out past the bookcases toward me—grasping breaths, like those of a severe asthmatic. I had fallen asleep listening to this rhythm, and now was waking up to it, relieved I could still hear it. How did Glen do this night after night? Was he, too, listening closely in case it stopped?

If I went back to sleep, maybe I'd wake up okay. Or I could get up and drink a glass of orange juice, and put down a few vitamin C. Maybe my throat was just dry. Maybe it had something to do with having been on a plane.

I tapped Ryan on the shoulder. He continued to snore. I pulled on his ear. He opened his eyes.

"We have to go home."

He was up on one elbow, looking at me. "What?"

"I have a cold."

"So?"

"So, Lou's immune system is a shambles, and she's got all this phlegm in her throat, never mind the actual tumours, and what if she gets my cold, and it clogs up her airway—"

"She won't get your cold."

"We can't take that chance. Listen. Can you hear her breathing?"

We were whispering furiously. Ryan put his hand on my head.

"Go back to sleep. You'll feel better when you wake up."

"I've been awake for an hour."

"What do you want me to do?"

"Can we go find a Starbucks or something?"

His faint, reddish eyebrows rose. "I thought you were against Starbucks."

There had been a battle in a Toronto neighbourhood over a Starbucks moving in across the street from a family café that had been around for decades. I saw them as predatory. But now I was in their backyard, and under the circumstances, I could not have cared less where my coffee came from.

We dressed and crept out of the apartment, grabbing a set of keys on the way. The streets were quiet, and though it was overcast, glowing in the morning light.

"Maybe we'll find the sexy mermaid," I said. Glen had told us about the controversy when Starbucks had first ventured north from Seattle. "The mermaid had cleavage," he said, "and people freaked out." She'd been covered up, or rendered less busty. Apparently, there was still one location with the old logo, a kind of unofficial landmark.

We walked to Burrard and turned toward False Creek. Nothing but apartment buildings—building after building. It was a boxy city, I thought. But the surroundings were dazzling enough that you could see how the city itself had taken a back seat. I remembered that Glen or Lou had mentioned a little ferry below the Burrard Street Bridge. "Let's see if we can find it."

Ryan shrugged. Okay. He was still half-asleep. Sure enough, a little boat was puttering along beneath the bridge. Two bucks each to ride to Granville Island and back. We scrambled aboard, and the captain pushed off. We were his only passengers. Neither my reading nor education had yet made me aware of this lonesome, misty scene's reminiscence of the River Styx and Dante's *Inferno*. To me, we'd wandered into a storybook. The captain let us off at the dock on the other side, next to a market building, bright and inviting.

Inside, we walked past dangling coils of sausage, bright red salmon on beds of ice, pyramids of melons and lettuce heads, vast wheels of cheese. I turned my head this way and that. I breathed in a heady potion of smells. In a world of such abundance, how could anything really be the matter?

AT THE FAR END OF THE MARKET, RYAN AND I FOUND A café. We bought coffee and croissants and sat by the window, watching gulls fly over False Creek.

"She'd rather have you here," Ryan said.

"I have to tell her."

"Sure, if you want. But I know what she'll say."

I frowned.

"Just don't be kissing her," he said. "Or sharing your toothbrush."

"Very funny."

What she wanted wasn't the point. I was contagious. I didn't have an answer. We got up to explore further, and I felt that hunger that happens in a new place, for seeing:

I had to peer around every corner, walk down every passage-way. The building was full of stalls and little shops tucked away in half-hidden alcoves. Paintings, knitted things, hand-made soap. In a store filled with delicately carved boxes and Asian handicrafts, I saw a silver ball hanging on a thin black cord. It felt heavy in my palm, and the shopkeeper told me to hold it to my ear, and jiggle. It chimed lightly, sonorously. I smiled.

I read the tag. It was a harmony ball, something to do with inner balance and peace. It cost eight dollars. "I can afford that," I told Ryan.

"You might want to wait before getting a souvenir."

"Not for me. For Lou. Like a talisman."

Why did I suddenly want to buy her things? I'd brought her a gift from Toronto—a beige hat that had prompted her to crouch behind the big plant in their living room and pre-tend she was on safari. Traditionally, the gifts we'd given each other had been homemade. We presented one another with modest, personalized crafts, like the jelly-bean-jar desk lamp Louisa had unveiled back at my apartment in January. My birthday gift.

"You made this? Yourself?" I was recalling the clown that sat on a shelf dangling its legs: a fabric body over wooden blocks. Very cute, but Lou had admitted sheepishly that her stepmother had been the source of the design, and the bulk of the sewing. The only part I knew Lou had done herself was the miniature "book" pinned to the clown's felted hand. On its cover was written, in tiny printing, "*Brow*, an auto-biography by Anita Lahey." A reference to my bushy eyebrows, and the insecurity that had always gone with them. I played along, laughing. But I was hurt, whether more about being teased, or about her not really putting much heart into the gift, I wasn't sure.

The lamp, she'd assured me, was entirely her own work. "And you wouldn't believe how many jelly beans it took to fill that jar!"

"What if I eat them all while I'm working?"

"Refills are on your own dime."

Now here I was, buying her gifts left and right. On the way back to the little ferry boat, the silver ball tucked in a little box in my pocket, I remembered my throat. I swallowed. It wasn't so bad, not nearly as raw as when I'd woken up. Maybe we could stay.

GLEN AND LOU OWNED A JUICER, WHICH THEY KEPT under the kitchen sink and talked about as though it were a miracle machine.

"It's cool," I said, eyeing it with suspicion.

They chiefly used it to make carrot juice, which had been a key ingredient in the macrobiotic diet Lou had adopted that fall. The idea was to purify her system, give it the chance to repair itself. I got why Lou tried macrobiotics, and likewise Glen's willingness to go along. Louisa didn't think her new doctor believed she would get well. And the fact was, conventional medicine wasn't cutting it. Nor did it give her any sense that her own efforts, in whatever form, would influence anything at all.

So Lou had decided she would keep doing what this doctor suggested, even when yet another chemo was proposed to replace the Interferon—one that would be much more powerful than anything she'd taken before. But she also began to look further afield. For months she'd been injecting herself with a mistletoe extract that was meant to stimulate her immune system. I was dubious about the treatment's potential but impressed that she had the gumption to give herself needles. She took up art therapy, too, and when a nutritionist proposed a macrobiotic diet, she thought: Why not? The diet was one more tool she picked up and used.

Meanwhile, Lou had heard about a study on a melanoma vaccine at the John Wayne Cancer Institute in California. She'd asked her former and current oncologists to send letters, along with her medical history, to the doctors in charge, pleading her case to take part. They reviewed her documentation and invited her down for some tests.

Lou and Glen flew to California in late January 1994, not long after she visited Toronto on my birthday and less than two weeks after the Northridge earthquake that wracked Los Angeles. It lasted twenty seconds, collapsed a freeway overpass, and caused seventy-two deaths and more than nine thousand injuries. Those people didn't have a chance to even look for an escape route, I remember thinking: death landed, literally, upon them.

California was a revelation—and a holiday. Lou had cousins there whom she hadn't seen for years; she and Glen stayed with them. Between appointments, they went to Disneyland. Glen took a picture of Louisa with Mickey Mouse, which I keep a copy of in an old photo album. She's wearing a khaki jacket and a navy hat with a curled-up brim. She has one arm flung around Mickey. The other's a flourish in the air, as though she's saying to an audience, *Ta da!* Her smile is wide, her cheeks rosy. No one, seeing the photo, would guess there was anything amiss.

Bad news: the California doctors didn't want her on their study. No vaccine for Louisa. But their reason for turning her away was astonishing. Her audio journal entry on the trip explains it best:

Well, I don't believe it. I don't believe what has happened. First of all, I had three doctors looking at me like I was a freak. And then they announced, and I had always known this, that I had an unusual case of melanoma. But these men are going right back to the source, and they're saying, "We don't know if you have melanoma." Which would prove why nothing has worked!

I've always had an atypical type melanoma. It took about ten years and nine pathology reports to figure out that I had melanoma. What they're telling me now is that it might not even be. My mother is psychic, I swear. She keeps saying, she has always been saying, "I don't think you have melanoma. I think they're gonna find that it's not melanoma." And we'd go, "Ya, Mom, okay," like she's crazy.

This changes everything. For a period last year, I had chemotherapy, and in that period for the first five months I was doing very well, and they thought I was gonna be in remission. And all of a sudden things slowed down, and my mental attitude changed, and I went, basically, down into the dumps. This man said that if we have a mixture of melanoma and something else, some other cancer, some disease, well it makes complete sense. Because, what happened was, the chemo killed the melanoma, like it was supposed to, but then we gave it a bit of a chance, because I had some surgery to check if the cancer was gone, and in that meantime the other cancer had the chance to replace the tumour. And so now I wasn't dealing with melanoma anymore, I was dealing with something else.

He's incredible. He's so optimistic. I don't know. Maybe it's just this man. His name is Dr. F–. Just a super guy. Very kind looking. And I can't believe what he told me. He's looking at it as a challenge. He's saying, "Wow, this could be a lot of things, and therefore, there's a lot of possibilities to getting you a cure. We know that it's not a typical melanoma because it hasn't killed you yet, frankly."

So, what he wants me to do is go back to Vancouver, and I'm gonna have some lumps removed and he actually wants me to send him one, and he's going to put it through pathology at his lab. And they're gonna decide if they think it's melanoma, in which case I may be able to go forward with the vaccine. But if it isn't, there's a whole world of things we could do and—I was just so, astounded, I guess, by what he had said to me, I started talking, about my doctor and how it felt so gloomy, like I was gonna die, and I was being [pause] stupid to be optimistic. And he said no, he said it's often true that some doctors see cancer as the "glass is half empty." They always see it as the glass is half empty. He said, "But here we're working on the top of technology. We can see it as the glass is half full. The glass is half full. It hasn't gone into your organs. It's not in your brain." It's only on the outside, and it's been that way ever since I got it, and because of that there's possibilities. There's actually possibilities, that I could live longer than the next five years.

And I can't tell you what that feels like. You know, I always went to the doctor, and I don't know, I never thought that he really believed that I could get better. And this man is looking at this as an opportunity to find, you know, more about my cancer and an atypical case. This is really a chance at my life. His science and my life. This isn't some quack telling me this, this is a very educated doctor who knows that it's possible. And I can't tell you what pressure that takes off me. I don't know what's gonna come of this, but I know this gives me a new way to look at things. I've always tried to be so positive, but now I feel like I have something really to be positive about.

You know, in cancer videos I've watched there's one man who said, "I decided if I was going to my grave, I certainly wasn't walking there. They were gonna have to drag me there." And I don't think they're even going to have to drag me there. I think there's real hope for the future. That's a feeling I haven't had in a really long time, and it feels really good.

There'd been no mention of California since the incident when Louisa had nearly stopped breathing—since the discovery of those tumours constricting her throat. I wanted to ask, and, at the same time, I didn't. I remembered the silver ball in my coat pocket. I left Glen and the juicer and went and got it. Lou shook it next to her ear and smiled. "It's perfect. I love it. Thanks." She hung it around her neck and leaned in for a careful hug.

Glen got to work feeding long, fat carrots into the juicer, which roared as it consumed them. As he pressed the orange stubs down into the blades, I cringed. I thought of lumber mills and logs, terrible accidents, pools of blood mixed with sawdust on the floor. I turned away—God forbid I conjure disaster—and noticed a list on the fridge.

"That's for the diet," said Lou. These were the acceptable foods. Barley. Brown rice. Squash. Carrots (of course). Fish. Nuts and seeds. Beans. Bulgur.

"What's bulgur?"

"A kind of grain. It's kind of blah. I'm not supposed to eat much meat."

"But now she eats whatever she can," said Glen. "It's more important that she eat something than follow the diet."

"It's hard. I'm not hungry. I make myself eat."

Lou sat down carefully at the round table in the kitchen alcove. She had the bag of pills. Glen brought a glass of thick orange liquid to the table, as well as a little white porcelain bowl and a porcelain rod.

I lit up. I knew what these were called: a mortar and pestle. I'd encountered these in stories now and then, being used by the characters within—I'd imagined them but never seen them in real life. "Is that for crushing the pills? Can I do it?"

"Be my guest," said Glen.

He handed me the little rod and bowl. It was so simple and ingenious. And weighty. This was the kind of thing I imagined both my grandmothers had kept in their kitchens as a basic, necessary tool. Ryan had joined us. He caught my eye. I was acting the way the other kids and I had in elementary school, when we would take turns trying out our classmate Jan's crutches at recess. I had told Ryan how friendly and patient Jan was, and how ashamed I'd become, years later, of our behaviour: we "able-bodied" kids treating the crutches Jan needed for walking like cool toys. Using a mortar and pestle would hardly be a novelty if you were crushing pills several times a day for your very sick girlfriend.

Lou said, "You can be in charge of the pills the whole time you're here." They set about explaining what was what. There was an orange pill, and a green one, and one that was white but a different colour on the inside. One was the cortisol steroid (which was supposed to help with nausea and pain, and even tumour-shrinkage); one was the anti-nausea medication that went with the chemo; one was the Tylenol 3, for pain. There were more.

"I can mix them all together?"

"That's the idea."

Mortar in one hand, pestle in the other, I twisted and pressed. The rod scraped and pinged against the bowl's interior. The pills broke into pieces, which I gleefully pulverized into a chalky powder, Louisa's magic dust. Its magic was weak. It couldn't blind a demon or douse a dragon's fire. At best, as night crept on, it would dampen her pain. Her breaths would deepen. She'd slip into a not-quite-sweet medicinal sleep.

SIXTEEN

A Chemo Cut

LOU PULLED HER HAIR FROM THE BRUSH AND LAID BOTH side by side on the sun-yellow comforter. They waited between us, the brush next to my leg, the hair next to hers. Her green Care Bear called Lucky, with the one winking eye, who had accompanied her on at least half a dozen hospital stays, was propped against a pillow behind us. I hadn't seen him since she'd moved out west, and I could swear he looked older and wiser, like he'd witnessed things that most stuffed toys never have to see.

The apartment was quiet. Ryan had gone with Glen to Safeway to buy Lou some popsicles to soothe her throat: the tri-colour kind that looked like a rocket ship. "High maintenance!" Ryan had said triumphantly. It was his favourite indictment of Lou. She pretended to be offended.

"So, I know what popsicles I like."

"I like banana," I said.

"Gross."

I started pushing the hair around on the yellow fabric, smoothing it out, holding it to the light. The sun seemed to give it life, the redness brightening strand by strand. People used to create jewellery from the hair of the dead and wear it as a symbol of mourning. Our hair will outlive us, I thought, simply by the fact that it is already dead. How depressing is that? "Imagine finding this in your brush every day for a month," I said.

"It won't last a month. It'll be long gone."

My eyes on hers answered: *This sucks*. Hers replied: *You have no idea*.

She looked into her lap. Her legs were bare: she was working up the energy to finish getting changed. We were going to Stepho's for dinner, her and Glen's favourite Greek restaurant, and Lou wanted to wear jeans. Her thighs were milky, dappled with orange. But they were no longer her legs. They were broom handles with skin.

Her hands in her lap, meanwhile, were puffed up, almost shapeless. The steroids did that. She and Glen constantly wrapped and rewrapped tensor bandages around them to keep the swelling down. It only partly worked.

I turned my eyes back to the hair in my hand. When she lifted her head from the pillow in the morning, a tangled layer stayed behind. It would just fall away. Let go. It collected on her shoulders throughout the day. You don't feel it losing hold, she told me, and then you look down at the brush and the bristles are full, or you absent-mindedly run a hand through your hair and discover a patch of scalp.

I remembered a long-ago speech she gave, about being a redhead. She'd spoken of being teased, and of the agony of sunburns. Sitting there in her Vancouver bedroom, nine years into our friendship, four years into her life with cancer,

I had yet to ask her what it was really like: having red hair. I knew nothing of the gruesome history of redheads, who were once routinely burned at the stake or buried alive and whose bodies were pillaged for their supposedly poisonous fat. I'd sat through enough John Hughes films—seen enough Molly Ringwald, adorned with super-cool, iron-red hair, sticking it to the rich kids, defiantly creating her prom dress from scraps—to get another idea, an idea of redheads as less destructible than the rest of us. Less vulnerable to the hazards of life on earth.

"What are you going to do? About your hair, I mean."

"I don't know."

"If you get it cut off, it's like 'Fuck it. I don't need it. Who cares?'"

"Maybe." She was only half listening. "They're pretty pathetic-looking aren't they?"

"What?"

"My legs."

I was still staring at them. I looked up. "Not pathetic. But you sure better not start complaining about your fat thighs."

"Anita, I don't know if I can do this."

"That's okay. We can stay in. Ryan and I can go pick food up."

"No, not dinner. This." She waved her hands over herself, her legs, her front, her head. "I don't even know how to describe it. I'm…tired."

"That's totally understandable. Of course you're tired."

"I haven't told you what happened."

My hands were gripping the side of the bed next to my knees. I was looking at my own legs now, sturdy and meaty, a little more meaty than I would have liked. I turned so I could watch her face as she spoke. But she dropped her own gaze, so all I saw was the slope of her nose, the freckles on her forehead. "Tell me."

She brushed her palms down her thighs. "It's stupid. It shouldn't bother me so much. It's my pride. I know that, but I can't shake it."

On the balcony earlier I'd seen two container ships anchored way out in English Bay. No movement, not even a gentle bobbing, was perceptible. They were like cut-outs pasted on the waves, lumpy, grey, and slightly askew. I wondered how far they'd travelled, and what the crew was doing now. Were they on the ships? Had they come ashore?

In the hospital, Lou was saying. The bathroom. The toilet was really low. There was nothing to hold.

I wasn't sure where she was leading. Then it hit home. She got stuck. Trapped on the toilet seat. Her legs were so weak she couldn't stand; she'd had to call Glen in to help. "I was—" She was holding the bear now; she was pressing the bear against her forehead. "If I can't even go to the bathroom myself—"

I placed a hand on her shoulder. "But you can now."

"So much for romance."

"Oh, you guys are so past all that. You have this—you have something I don't even know how to describe. I don't know what it is. It's amazing."

"It was so mortifying. I can't get over it."

"Give it time."

She shook her head. The green bear went with it, back and forth.

THERE WAS A LINEUP OUTSIDE STEPHO'S. I WAS READY TO say we should go somewhere else, but Lou just leaned against the wall. I worried that her legs would give out. Her jeans billowed about their thinness like capes.

After an agitating fifteen-minute wait, we were led to our table. Lou pulled me aside and whispered a request. I walked to the washroom, entered a stall, and hovered above the toilet seat. Low, medium, or high? I sat and stood, sat and stood, trying to imagine doing so with pipe cleaners for legs. Would I make it back up? I planned for the day when we'd laugh about the night Louisa turned me into her bathroom scout. I planned for it hard.

When I returned to the table, they were all talking about how, tomorrow, we'd take the ferry to Victoria and spend the night. "And while we're there," I said, "we'll find someone to chop off your hair." I grinned to indicate I was joking. Half joking.

"You're right," she said. Then Glen and Ryan got involved, and the four of us started to trash-talk her cancer. Before the tzatziki and pita arrived, the haircut had become a ceremony, a performance: we'd all be there, scripts and props at the ready. By the time we got on to how tough she'd look, how skater-boy, the effect she'd achieve with her blue paisley bandana and super-short, red-hot crop, everyone was convinced. It made sense. It was the only way.

WE SAT IN A CUBBYHOLE OF A SHOP ON PENDER STREET IN Chinatown. The walls were lined with foam heads, some bald, others adorned with blue, brown, black, red, and yellow wigs. Some curled, some straight. Spiked, piled, beehived. Long and shiny and far too real. A woman had marched into the back to fetch the one Lou ordered a couple of weeks back.

"What colour will it be?" I'd asked on the way there. We were all tucked into the Tercel. The wig shop was our pit stop en route to the ferry terminal at Tsawassen.

"You're joking," said Ryan.

"I'm serious."

"It's red," said Lou, not at all surprised by the question.

She knew who I was thinking about: Isabel. They'd shared a room at Princess Margaret Hospital in Toronto for a few days. Isabel had been on tough cancer drugs. She was bald. When her hair had started to go, she'd bought a wig: black as ink. Isabel's real hair was brown, but she'd always longed for a head full of night. "I had to get something out of this," she told Louisa. Then she told the story of the day she stepped off a bus into a fierce wind that took the hair right off her head. She stood there, smooth-scalped and stunned, watching her cool black wig flip-flop down the street. She thought this was hilarious. So did Louisa. They laughed themselves silly in their beds. Cancer-bonding; that's what they were doing. I hoped I succeeded in hiding, deep down inside my perfectly healthy body, that I actually felt left out.

We faced a mirror. My hair fell heavy and straight around my ears. It had never occurred to me before: What do they use to make wigs? Where does the hair come from?

"I think it's a mix," said Lou. "Part synthetic."

"Really? Like what, polyester or something?"

"I don't know. The real ones are a lot more expensive. They last longer but—" She shrugged. I was glad she didn't finish the sentence.

"I'm having a weird thought."

"What else is new."

"Seriously, they could have used your own hair."

Lou looked at me as if to say, "You're kidding." But I couldn't stop.

"Then it would be the exact right colour. What kind of red are they giving you?"

"Well, they saw me. I told them I wanted it the same."

"Hmm."

"They said they'd do their best. I gave them a picture, too."

Now we were both worried. Way to go, Anita. Excellent work. When the wig arrived Lou struggled with it. She was sore, and tired.

"It takes practice," the saleswoman said. "Don't worry."

The wig was a solid, dark red, slightly more metallic than Lou's. It was a flawless bob with impressively even bangs. I liked it and hated it at the same time. I focused on the like side of the equation, going so far as to call it "perfect," asking myself why I suddenly thought Louisa was too fragile for the truth.

Or maybe I'd realized that some "truths" aren't all that important.

THE SALON IN THE VICTORIA EATON CENTRE WAS CALLED the Cutting Edge, or something like that. The man at the counter wore black plants and a black shirt. His choppy dark hair glistened with product. His hands made me think of little birds—twitchy, restless. Next to him, Lou, with her bandana twisted tightly around her head, her cheeks bulging, appeared almost earthy. Not slick. Not hip.

We tried to explain. He smiled. I thought, *He's cool. He gets it.*

"A cut is thirty-two dollars. We wouldn't charge you for the blow-dry."

Thirty-two dollars was a meal out. Ferry tickets for the four of us. A new long-sleeved shirt from the Gap. "That's a lot for hair that's just going to fall out," Lou said. "Is there some way to get some kind of discount?"

"A cancer discount," Ryan said.

"Yeah," said Lou, perking up. "A chemo cut."

We all laughed. Except the man. "Maybe you want to skip the cut," he said, his hands taking flight. "If it's going to be gone that fast, why not just leave it?"

As we walked away I caught his eye. If I were a different kind of person, I'd have given him the finger.

We rode the elevator to the third floor and found salon number two. We approached the dark-haired woman at the counter and told her the score. She didn't bat an eye. "I can give you a kids' cut. Eleven bucks."

We were so grateful we all piled into the salon, into her realm of kindness. The salon leaned more toward a First Choice than a Giorgio's: lit like a movie star's dressing room, one long wall lined with mirrors and swivelling chairs. It smelled sharply of product. Lou sat quietly and straight-backed in a blue plastic smock while Glen chatted with the hairdresser about their favourite local restaurants—Pagliacci's especially, where all the dishes were named after Hollywood stars. Meanwhile, Ryan was squeezing between chairs and fixtures, crouching and twisting to get a better angle with his camera, taking photographs as though we were on a weekend holiday: two young couples on the lookout for adventure.

Lou widened her eyes, flattened her palms against her oversized cheeks and shaped her lips into a shocked O. She was hamming it up. Ryan focused and clicked. Focused and clicked.

The hairdresser paused between each snip, dangling the scissors like a pair of crossed swords. With each whirr and snap, I held my breath. On the chair next to Lou I'd laid out a series of navy-blue ribbons. My job was to collect her rich red hair as it dropped from her scalp, divide it by length and tie it into bundles. The growing piles of cuttings shimmered against the chair's vinyl covering, long and short, gingered and mulled. Snip, snip. I watched each finger-full fall away.

We were saving her hair on the off chance that it would grow back a different colour. We'd heard stories about this happening. It's one thing to be born with, say, brown hair. You learn to take comfort in its soft, mulchy blahness. It's another to have brownness thrust upon you.

I threw out a question. "All of it?"

"As much as you can."

"No problem."

The hairdresser was older than us, thirtyish, her own hairdo long and black, down to the chest. She parted Lou's hair in places and peered down, doctor-like, to survey the resident obstructions: four or five wide lumps—some of them split and rimmed with puss—that protruded as high as an inch or more from her scalp.

When we'd warned her about these she'd waved a hand in the air and said, "Don't worry. I'll be careful." She seemed so sure, it would have been insulting to insist. Now, with the lumps in her sights, she betrayed nothing. Neither shock nor disgust. Not even dismay. She passed me a fresh cutting—she was thoughtful enough to try to catch the longer strands before they fell to the floor. I could have gripped her by the shoulder. *This doesn't faze you at all? You think this is normal?*

For years I resented the time we spent in the mall that day: we'd turned precious hours over to a generic, indifferent setting. Now, though, I love the memory of that place and the view it provides: of an ordinary salon in which I see Lou and me, the men we most cared about, and a compassionate stranger, laughing and goofing off, doing something that no passerby catching our reflections in the mirrors would ever have imagined to be important.

The stylist lifted her fingers through Lou's partly chopped hair, mussing it. In a magazine such a cut would be filed under *sassy*. A little gel and it'd graduate to *chic*.

"It'll look good on you," she said. "Trust me."

LOUISA WAS STILL FLYING—WE ALL WERE, AFTER WE LEFT the hair salon. There's no real grade to what I would call the "fuck cancer" high: when you're up, you're up.

We decided to walk around downtown Victoria. Glen and Ryan went one way, Lou and I another, wending our way down Government Street. We soon found ourselves in a store filled with quilts and pillows and pottery. The place had a hushed quality, like a museum, which I could feel us shattering with our buzz.

In the back, hanging singly along the wall, were some formal dresses. They made me think of the shop in Village Square in downtown Burlington that Lou had always liked: Promises and Lace. She reached out to touch one. The bandana was tied artfully around her choppy cut.

"This is it," she said, with surprising energy. It was made of a delicate fabric in a shade resembling old parchment paper.

"What?"

She fingered a hem. "It's the dress you should get married in."

I rolled my eyes. "I'm not getting married."

"When you do, though. It's perfect. It's…unconventional."

I shrugged. "I may never get married."

"You won't marry Ryan?"

"I don't know. I've never thought about it." A lie. I wouldn't, I didn't think. Not because of him, just because. "Anyway, you know how I hate dressing up."

"You need to get over that."

"It just seems so, I don't know, superficial. Why can't we just *be*?"

"There's nothing wrong with looking good, Anita. It's not evil."

I let out a sigh. Was this really the time to address my hang-ups? "Louisa, I have no interest in weddings. You know that."

She laughed. She thought I was just being difficult. "I know you won't do frills," she said. "That's cool. But this one doesn't have any. Just look at it." She had that tinge of awe in her voice that she was so good at. It was the voice that once had me believing she and Jon had shared the same dream, the voice that got me half counting on the messages coming to me through my horoscope.

She rubbed a sleeve between her thick, swollen fingers. I had seen those fingers, those hands, writing and gesturing and clenching and fidgeting before me for so many years they were part of my landscape. Now, I wouldn't recognize them. She turned to me. "It's like it was made for you. You should try it on."

I made myself look at the dress, really look. The neckline was scooped, the waist came in below the breasts, Anne Boleyn–style. The skirt was neither straight nor excessively full. The sleeves, gently laced, had a slight puff at the shoulders. The more I looked, the more I thought Lou might be right. If I had to wear a dress, this would be the one.

I turned the price tag. Yikes. I yanked my hand away. "I can't try this on. Look at me. They'll know I'm never gonna buy it." And who were we kidding? I wasn't a dress girl. It would look dumb.

"So what? Come on. It'll be fun."

Frustrated, I thought, *If I did get married in this dress you wouldn't get to see it anyway.* Then: *Holy shit. Thank God I didn't say that out loud.*

I was suddenly weary. I watched the energy drain out of Louisa too. It went down fast, like there was something sucking it out through her heels.

We left the store. A couple of blocks away, we found the guys in a linen shop where Ryan was hunting down the family tartan. Lou lifted a blue tam off a hat rack. She tilted it sidelong on her head, and gently sat herself in a large wing-back chair. She put her head back and closed her eyes. The most prominent tumour in her neck jutted out, stretching the skin. The regret appeared out of nowhere. The racks of clothing, the salespeople, the other browsers faded. Why wouldn't I try on the damn dress? For a few minutes I could have let her imagine I'd walk down the aisle some-day. I could even have imagined it myself.

LEAVING TOWN, WE TOOK THE SCENIC ROUTE ALONG Dallas Road. We stopped at Mile Zero of the Trans-Canada Highway, by the statue of Terry Fox. Ryan and I got out of the car to get a closer look. I considered the curly-haired boy in the statue, then my weakened friend in the Tercel. Fox had run a marathon every day for months, and I'd always wondered what compulsion had made this possible. I didn't think it was anything so straightforward as that he was trying to outrun the bad cells.

I walked back to the car, waving to Lou as I approached. She waved back. I lifted both hands high over my head and waved in giant arcs, as if from a far shore. Ahoy there! She grinned. She sat up straight and raised her thick hand wrapped in the tensor, propping her elbow in the open win-dow. She turned the hand ever so slowly, left, right, left. The regal wave. Farewell, Victoria. We're blowing this popsicle stand. I slipped my fingers into the door handle and pulled.

SEVENTEEN

The Perfect Meringue

A THICK MIST SETTLED, THROUGH WHICH FAT, WEIGHTY droplets would spill at intervals. In winter, Lou told me, it'd been like this for months. She'd never gone so long without seeing the sun.

We sat in the nook, scrunched close around a corner of the kitchen table. In the week we'd been here I'd grown fond of this spot. The flowered makeup bag, mortar and pestle, and an empty juice glass, stained orange, were pushed aside: medication, check. I'd tightened the tensors on her hands and feet; they were tidy and snug. She was still in what passed for pyjamas: a loose T-shirt of Glen's and her old pink track pants, faded to near white. Her choppy haircut stood out over her head in jaunty clumps. Its wonkiness cheered me. So far the full sections concealed the bare patches *and* the tumours.

We'd slid some photos Lou and Glen had just gotten developed out of a white envelope and were sifting through. Lou set aside a photo of Glen and his sisters. Beneath it was one of Lou in Glen's blue bathrobe, sitting at this same white table, in front of a lemon meringue pie, grinning fiercely. This was a month or so ago. Before the steroids, but not before she'd started growing thin. Her hair, still shoulder length, was askew, unbrushed. Her cheeks sunk in, and her eyes seemed to pop forward, round and bright.

"There it is," she said. "The famous pie."

"Oh yeah." I remembered a phone call now, triumphant. Something to do with Glen's mom and meringue.

"I said I loved making lemon pie and she gave me that look she has—ugh, she's so skeptical. I get angry just thinking about it. She said"—Lou sat up straight and eyed me darkly—"'Well, I've seldom seen meringue done right. Never mind the crust. Baking is a skill, you know.'"

"You're kidding."

"She's convinced I'm a flake. She *was* convinced."

Louisa picked up the photo gingerly, by a corner, and pointed at the pie. "It took three tries to get it right."

"The meringue looks like snow drifts."

"I've never heard her praise anything so much. I almost wanted her to go back to normal and pick it apart." She tossed it back on the pile, sat back, and crossed her arms, her swollen hands hidden inside the beige bandages. "Since then, I can do no wrong."

"Huh. I thought you were supposed to win a *man* through his stomach, not win his mother that way."

Lou laughed. "Mrs. Mackay is a special case."

The phone rang. It was Louisa's mom, calling to invite us to meet her for church in the morning, and then come by for brunch. Lou put her hand over the receiver to ask me.

"Sure. Whatever you like."

But after she hung up I said, "Church? Remember what happened last time?"

Since they'd moved, Lou's mom had been trying out different churches. She'd finally found one she thought she liked, with a pleasant choir and a thoughtful priest. Lou joined her for Mass one Sunday. But a different priest delivered the homily this time.

"He was all fire and brimstone," Lou had told me. She'd left the church crying. Her mother had run out after her.

The priest had pronounced that a sin was a sin and if we didn't follow God's laws we'd pay the consequences, if not here, in the afterlife. I wanted to know: What kind of sins did he mean? Real sins, such as hurting someone deliberately, or what the Catholic Church declared to be sins, such as having sex outside of marriage or using birth control? The whole enchilada, Louisa-shacked-up-with-her-boyfriend said, her voice jumping an octave. I asked her, But why take it to heart? You know that stuff is crap. She interrupted me. But is it? How do we know for sure? He's just one priest, I told her. Some of them get off on scaring people. I can't help it, she said. I feel so vulnerable.

I feel so vulnerable.

I made myself think it: she'd come close to death. The "judgment" this priest felt compelled to threaten people with was, to her, no longer abstract.

Now she was saying, "I feel a lot better since then, about all that. There's something I should show you. Give me your arm?"

"You okay?"

"Yes fine, it's just getting up. I need to start doing some exercises. To get the muscle back."

She turned in her chair, gripped the table with one hand and my forearm with the other, and carefully stood.

"You could even just do some leg lifts while you're sitting down. That might help."

"You're right. It doesn't have to be a lot."

"Someone at the hospital should have given you tips." I felt frustration rising. Practical care. Common sense. Where was it? I don't think either of us knew about "wasting" or what it signified.

"Yeah, well." She smiled and turned. "I'll be right back."

She moved through the kitchen as slowly as if she were feeling her way. Past the fridge she turned left and out of sight. I sat with the photos. The shot of her with the lemon pie was still on top. Since when was Louisa into competitive homemaking? Since when did she consider meringue a major accomplishment? I took the photo and held it up. The pie, in all its decadent perfection, said, *Check it out, Louisa made me, yeah, the one you all think is so sick and so flakey. Ha. Flakey. Get it?* I kicked myself. It made total sense: a skill she could master. A challenge she could meet. It was a kind of proof.

When Lou returned she passed me a handful of cue cards. I splayed them like a poker hand and pulled one out. It was peach-coloured and had a quote from Psalms printed on it: "Your word is a lamp to guide me and a light to my path. Teach me your ways, O Lord, and lead me along a safe path." The card was also stamped with a circle containing the phrase "Unity in Jesus," like a brand. I picked out a yellow card—not bright but deep, like mustard. It bore a quote from Exodus: "I will send an angel ahead of you to protect you as you travel and to bring you to the place which I have prepared."

Cripes. "Where'd you get these?"

"Ida."

A beat. "Ida?"

"You know, my grandmother's friend…"

"Yeah. I remember."

Ida was one of the sharper memories I had of a March Break trip I'd once taken with Louisa, her mother and brothers, to visit her mother's mother, who Lou and her brothers called Nanan. She lived in a pretty, hilly, New Hampshire town. We'd spent an afternoon wandering around the campus of Dartmouth, an Ivy League university that Lou and I were determined, somehow, to attend, despite two obvious obstacles: admittance and cost. We drank milkshakes in a diner downtown, bought T-shirts, and acted like we knew something about Cape Cod architecture. We also privately cracked jokes about her Nanan's friend Ida, who drove around with a "Jesus Loves You" bumper sticker on the back of her car.

I guessed, as I flipped through the prayer cards, that we weren't making fun of Ida anymore. "She sent you these?"

"After that episode at church. I was talking to Nanan, and Ida got on the phone. She made me feel a lot better."

"About God?"

"She said the priest was way off base. You only have to let Jesus in. It's crazy but I felt so much better after."

"That's good," I said. I was sure I didn't grimace. I hoped not.

"They're simple," she said. "They help."

"I'm glad."

CRAWLING INTO THE LIVING ROOM FUTON THAT NIGHT beside Ryan, I caught a vision of myself as a girl, rummaging through the bedclothes early in the morning, looking for my lost rosary beads. The sorrowful mysteries, how I'd tried to pray my way through them after Dad's heart attack, and during other family crises. *The Agony in the Garden.* There must be a part of me left that could still understand the need to reach for that place. I lay back and pulled the comforter up to my chin.

THE SUN WAS OUT, AND THE GRASS WAS SO GREEN IT looked wet. *Lush*, I thought. *This is what people mean by "lush."*

We were in a tony Vancouver neighbourhood, walking around a low brick church, looking for a way in that didn't involve a staircase. Lou was dressed smartly, in navy cotton pants with a short cream jacket over top. Her hair was thick, red and shimmering—neck-length. The wig. I'd helped her situate it carefully before we left. "It's time," she'd said. It looked flawless and rich. It also looked completely wrong, like she was in costume. But a stranger wouldn't know the difference. They'd never know this was Louisa trying like hell just to be Louisa.

"Mom hasn't really seen me like this. She's been away on a course."

"But she knows what happened."

"She knows." Lou hesitated. "I kind of toned it down."

"Lou."

"She has so much on her plate. I don't want—"

"Lou!"

"I just don't want to be one more thing she has to worry about."

"She's already worried, believe me. She's your mom."

"You're right. It's just—it's hard. She'll be shocked even to see me. She hasn't seen me walk."

We found a side door with only one step in front of it.

"Here," I said, holding it open for her. "And if the priest is a jerk we'll leave early. Right?"

"Right."

I followed her into the cool, dim room lined with polished pews. I breathed in. Candle wax, must, hint of incense. A few rows from the back, a woman with short, wavy red hair sat alone, shoulders straight, hands in her lap. She must have sensed us; she turned and waved, smiling. We slid in beside her. Lou hugged her and they immediately started whispering. Her mother reached up and took some strands of the wig between her fingers. On her face, a questioning look. More whispering. Nodding. *Oh*, I could see her thinking. *Oh*. She placed both hands around the back of Lou's neck and pulled her close.

I saw the padded kneeler tucked up by our feet and thought, I'll pray. I'd been trained for this, after all. I eased the kneeler down and let my knees fall to meet it. I propped my elbows on the back of the pew in front, folded my hands and rested my chin on my knuckles. My lids came down; the pews, Lou, her mom, the wig, disappeared. I imagined a vast, open space into which my thoughts, jostling those launched by millions of others, would sail, beneath a white flag of surrender.

Please, I began.

THE CONDO WAS BRIGHT AND CLEAN, LIKE THE ONE LOU and her mom had left behind in Toronto.

Lou's mom opened the fridge and began pulling things out. She handed me a bowl of chopped fruit and a container of yogurt. She passed Louisa a jug of freshly squeezed orange juice and turned away. I started—I nearly dropped my yogurt to grab the jug. Lou shook her head and lifted the juice, which she held in two hands. *Not too heavy*. We carried our cargo to the table, which was already laid out with plates, cutlery, and glasses. Her mom followed with a plate of cheese and crackers.

"I thought I'd fry some bacon and scramble eggs. How does that sound?"

I opened my mouth but Louisa cut me off. "It sounds delicious."

I eyed the feast already on the table. Lou would nibble at best. From the kitchen, her mom called, "So have you given up on the diet, Louisa?"

"Mostly. It was too much. It was stressing me out."

Her mom poked her head back into the room. "You've lost too much weight."

"I know."

Then the talk was of Lou's brothers, what was new with Glen (*Nothing much. You know he took a leave from Simon Fraser. Oh, yeah, you mentioned that. I hope he doesn't let it go entirely*), the course Lou's mom had just taken (*An inspiration!*), and my family. What was new? What was my sister planning to study at Queen's? And the all-important boyfriend?

Louisa jumped in. "They're moving to Ottawa in the fall! Ryan is going to teacher's college."

"And Anita?"

I shrugged. "I was going to have to leave the magazine anyway—they don't have funding to keep us another year. I can freelance. And I like the idea of living somewhere else. A new city."

"It's a big step, moving in."

I frowned. "I know. We only just made up our minds." The other morning, actually, walking back from the Granville Island ferry. I wasn't sure why I suddenly felt this was okay.

"Just don't expect roses every day," Lou's mom said. "Go into it with your eyes open."

I stretched the lids of both eyes back with my thumbs and forefingers. "I'll put toothpicks on the grocery list."

Lou beamed. "I'm so happy for them."

She'd told me this the night before, out on the balcony. We were long past her horror over my relationship with Ryan. Still, I was surprised by her enthusiasm. I had the distinct sense that behind it was relief: she'd been worried for me, but wasn't anymore.

Lou's mom, sprinkling salt on her eggs, said, "So." She passed the salt to me. "What have you heard from the handsome doctor in California?"

"I think they're still assessing," said Lou.

"I thought they knew."

"It was all uncertain."

"Have you called them?"

"They said they would be in touch."

"Well, I hope your doctor here gets off her ass and gets the information they have. What is she waiting for? Meanwhile, she still has you on that chemo."

"I go this week actually."

"Oh, Louisa."

"Mom, I have to do something."

"It's the wrong treatment."

"But it's something. I can't just do nothing."

"Maybe we need to get you back down to California. You can stay with your cousins, as long as you need to. You know they'd have you."

"I know." With the back of her fork, she pushed some egg around on her plate.

Her mom swallowed some juice. "You just tell me what you want to do, Louisa. Just say the word. We can try anything, anything at all."

"Thanks, Mom. You're the best." Lou leaned over and kissed her on the cheek. Her mom's eyes flashed across the table, my way, that same strange, endless blue as Louisa's.

Ocean broiling. She took Louisa's chin and looked at her straight. "Have some more eggs. Just a few forkfuls. You need your strength."

She saw everything: she knew. But if she seemed frightened, her daughter would be forced to comfort her. That would never happen. Not now, not ever. *Come to me. Eat this meal that I have prepared. I will give you rest.* I'd thought I was the one who saw what was going on in Louisa's head, as much as anyone could, except maybe for Glen. But Lou's mom's understanding went back to the day Louisa first laid eyes on this world, and to the months before that, when she was unseen but felt, fluttering and swishing, all of life before her.

Mrs. Prose leaned forward, elbows on the table, coffee mug raised. "So, what have you girls been up to? Tell me everything."

I pointed a fork at Lou. "Yesterday we spent hours admiring a picture of a pie."

"Oh yes, the famous pie. You know, I taught her everything she knows about meringue."

Lou smiled and dipped her fork into the fluffy yellow heap on her plate. Take the good and leave the bad. My dad was always saying this to me about church. Take what's worthwhile, forget the rest. The psalm came back to me, its simple spell.

I will both lie down and sleep in peace
for you alone, O Lord,
make me lie down in safety.

EIGHTEEN

A Serpent Came Down the Mountain

THE DAYS PASSED, FULL DAYS THAT TIRED ME OUT. I MAR-
velled at how much Lou seemed able to do. We checked out
UBC. We walked down the Robson Street strip, wandering
in and out of shops we couldn't afford. We ate at White Spot.

"It's no Swiss Chalet," I said to Lou.

"I know. But don't tell Glen."

The day we drove to Whistler, Louisa couldn't keep her
eyes open in the car. From the seat behind her I saw Glen
glance at her frequently, stealing his eyes from the winding
highway that skirts the mountains along the coast. Her
breathing was rough and irregular, as it sounded through
the night. I didn't know where to look: at the sheer rock
walls on one side, where occasionally you could see a blue
or red speck like a thumbtack in the stone (climbers, Glen
said, to my amazement); or out over the waters of Howe
Sound, where islands floated in mists, like the settings for
the secret palaces of ancients gods.

"Are you okay?" Glen asked.

"I'm fine."

"Are you sure?"

"I'm tired, that's all."

This conversation repeated itself as we passed Shannon Falls; as we neared the centre of Squamish, where we pulled into McDonald's; and again, beyond the local Squamish reserve.

"Are you sure you're okay?"

"I'm not planning to die this afternoon! Okay?"

Silence.

"I was just making sure."

"I'm just closing my eyes. Can't a person close their eyes?"

The previous evening, we'd been hanging around in the apartment when Lou suddenly said to Glen and me that she wanted us to read her journal after she was "gone": she was leaving it in our care and thought it was important for us both to read it. She was sitting in the padded lawn chair eating a tri-colour popsicle, the tensor around her hand starting to loosen. I avoided Glen's eye. That was nonsense, I said, she would still be writing in the journal years later— that same blue book, because she didn't seem able to fill it up. But I also told her, in the next breath, that of course I would read it, if, if, if—if that was what she wanted.

And so, there would come a summer day, on a later trip to Vancouver, when Glen and I would walk together into a downtown Kinko's. He'd have the heavy blue journal tucked under his arm. We'd proceed to a self-serve machine, where Glen would open the journal to the first page and turn it face down on the glass. A bright light, like a captured star, would slide across the glass. The machine would spit out a long sheet of paper covered in what would look just like Lou's scrawl, but of course would be merely a facsimile.

I'd pick up the paper knowing that her hand had never touched it.

A few days later I'd tuck my stack of sheets carefully into my suitcase, beneath rolled T-shirts and jeans. Glen would drive me to the airport. I'd bring all those recorded Louisa moods, those moments of anxiety and optimism translated into text, those plans and fears and solutions and ideas and uncensored emotions, home.

I HADN'T KNOWN WHISTLER WAS LIKE A SMALL TOWN nestled among mountains—nor that there were glaciers there. It was breathtaking, and surreal. As we strolled, Ryan and I looking up at the peaks and clouds, Glen explained the nuances: there was Whistler, and there was Blackcomb. Though Whistler was more famous, Blackcomb was the taller peak and had some tougher runs. Lou and I noticed a young guy on crutches. Then another, and another.

"Daredevils?" I asked.

"Or just rotten skiers," she said.

"Or they smoked too much dope," said Ryan.

On the way home we stopped, as planned, at Shannon Falls, a 335-metre waterfall just off Highway 99. Ryan and I hiked up the trail to the platform overlooking the high, narrow falls that twisted and turned in their powerful descent. An information panel there told the story of the two-headed sea serpent Sinulhkay, which, in Squamish tradition, slithered up and down these mountains so many times it carved a spillway from the rock.

Watching the water fall in great, tumbling bursts, I tried to picture the giant serpent twisting its way down the mountain, scraping the rock with its thick, leathery belly. Was it chasing after something, or on the run from a predator—

some creature even more magnificent? Even mythical beasts had things to fear. The serpent hadn't made the falls deliberately: they were evidence of its travels, a kind of memorial. Whether it'd been hunting, exploring, or fleeing, the effect was the same.

There would be no such rewriting of the landscape after our trip was over, no channel gouged out of the earth where we'd driven and sailed and walked. But it seemed there ought to be a trail at least, trodden through a different kind of wilderness by four pairs of footprints—faint, yet, if you knew what to look for, unmistakable.

Ryan went out onto a rock over the barrier, nearer the water. I walked back down the hill ahead of him, and found Glen and Lou lingering on the path.

"Hi," I said cheerfully. They nearly jumped. They looked at me with glossy eyes. "I'm sorry. Are you guys okay? I can go."

"No, don't," said Glen.

"We're great," said Lou. Her voice wavered. She wiped a hand over her cheek. One of her tensors had come loose.

"Let me fix that." I took her hand and began to unwind the elastic material.

"We're just so happy," said Glen. He turned to Lou. "How do we explain?"

"I just can't believe I'm back here," said Lou. "It's incredible. It just hit me all of a sudden. I'm so grateful."

"And you guys are here," Glen said, "and it's just awesome."

What had she said when she'd asked me to fly out here? "I had to make a choice. I could have let go, I knew I could have, but I didn't want to. I wasn't ready." I didn't know what that was like, nor to have seen her in that moment as Glen had, coming to that precipice and drawing back again. "It *is* awesome," I said, redundantly, helplessly. "It's wonderful."

Ryan came down the path and saw our faces. "What's wrong with everyone?"

We laughed, and wiped our eyes, and started toward the car.

IT WAS A WARM EVENING WITH NO RAIN. I HAULED THE reclining lawn chair outside so Lou and I could sit on the balcony. Glen and Ryan had gone to the arcade; we'd urged them to go. We'd been in Vancouver a week and a half, and our gallivanting was over. Lou would start her three-day round of chemo at the hospital in the morning. The day after it was finished, Ryan and I would fly home.

"It's good for Glen that you guys are here," she said. "He's usually just stuck with me."

"I'm sure he doesn't feel stuck. I'm sorry I ever doubted him."

"You had reason to. He was a dope." Her head fell back against the chair. "I was so thrilled to live on the seventeenth floor, with that view, and I hardly ever come out here." She shifted her head and jiggled her swollen feet. The concrete railing was so high that while sitting you couldn't see over it. I stood up and looked out at English Bay. It was broad and serene and unsatisfying in its indifference.

"Anita, I don't know if I can do it."

"Do what?"

"The drugs. They're so strong. They really knocked me out last time."

I could still hear the water moving, soft but insistent, and I thought of that old Blue Rodeo song about English Bay, and how the waves seemed to carry the singer's loneliness. Vancouver was misty and damp and dripping with sadness.

"But that was so soon after your other episode in the hospital. With your throat. You were weaker then."

"I don't know. I just—I don't want to lose the days. You're only here for a few more days."

"You can't skip it because *we're* here. What if it's helping?"

"But I'll lose those days."

"We've had so many wonderful days," I said.

"I know, you're right."

"It's okay. Don't worry. Get your treatment. Do what you have to do."

A few weeks earlier, Louisa had written what was to be the last entry in her journal, one of only a handful she'd put down in the blue book since more than a year before.

In this entry, her handwriting is markedly changed. As long as I'd known her she'd scrawled fat, round letters that leaned casually back, as if trying to look unconcerned. Here, the letters tip forward, slim and sure. It's as if she's found her source of strength, and it has run through her fingertips onto the page.

March 28, 1994   7:50 am

Why shouldn't this be the day?!!

I have worked as hard as I have been able to over the past 11 years to get over this disease—and I've done a great job.

Now this last couple have been a little much. But OK—I've dealt with them in the same manner. Like a winner. I have always dealt with this like I was going to beat it.

I know this happened to change the course of my life somehow. I know now that I have to do something useful & giving with all I have learned & continue to.

It's that one thing that Billy Crystal refers to in City Slickers—that one thing on the end of your finger that's the most important thing in life. I remember watching that video & being perplexed—what could it be?

LOVE—it's the people you love—that's it.

It's about giving or at least attempting to give that love to someone every day. Trying to make the world a better place. In every activity, our attitude determines where that energy goes.

That's it.

So today can be the day. I go forward with only love to give and forgive everyone who has ever hurt me.

I don't have the energy or the time to be looking back.

Only positive energy—for the future—my future— our future

only love—

Louisa

What could I say to this wonderful group of people that could ever adequately describe the feeling & power in it?? You people have more than added to, or been a part of, my life…you have been my life!!

When I read this now, I don't understand her use of the phrase "the future" to mean what we'd normally think it to mean. And I don't know that it was meant to imply "afterlife" either. What I do know is that, whatever it was to contain, Louisa—at least on the day she wrote this—was ready for it, okay with it, content.

RYAN WAS BACK AT THE APARTMENT AND I'D SENT GLEN there too—to rest, have a shower, eat. Louisa was two days into a harsher round of chemo than I'd ever seen her endure—or was she just weaker than ever?—and Glen had been sleeping in the room with her at the B.C. Cancer Agency. If you could call it sleeping. She woke frequently through the night with pain, or coughing. The phlegm problem had amplified. She had a supply of pressed cardboard trays into which she spat, which she and Glen had brought home with them after their last trip to the hospital. They'd made a game around the phlegm, becoming excited over a particularly large or gross specimen. We gleefully noticed that after she'd eaten a popsicle, the phlegm's colour matched.

By now she was virtually knocked out by the drugs, which she received continuously through an IV. She was awake, but barely able to open her eyes or speak. The coughing episodes continued. When one began, she might need me to pass her the tray, or hold it for her while she spat. After all the time I'd spent with her in hospital rooms over the years, this was a descent into debilitation that shocked me. I said goodbye to Glen and sat down across from her. Should I talk to her, or would she prefer peace and quiet? I knew she was capable of nodding, shaking her head, a word here or there. I remembered the conversation we'd had two nights before, when she told me she was afraid to come back in for the treatment.

"But what if it's helping?" I'd asked.

I have turned back to this moment many times over the years, to what Lou said about the drugs and how I responded, to the two of us sitting in the concrete cocoon of the balcony, the grey sky overhead and, out there, beyond the chunky, apartment-filled, western edge of downtown Vancouver, the calm of English Bay. Louisa had been looking for an out—for permission. She'd had enough. Yet I'd pushed her on.

Louisa lifted her arm, fumbled for the Vaseline tub from the table next to her and brought it carefully to her lap.

I started out of my chair. "Do you want a hand?"

She shook her head. No. I sat back down.

With difficulty, she lifted the white lid off the tub. She dipped in two fingers and scooped out a glob of jelly. This new chemo was causing her soft tissues to dry out, to crack and hurt. Her nostrils were raw and sore. The Vaseline would soothe them. As she raised her arm toward her face, she lost focus. It began to fall. She remembered what she was doing and began to lift it again. Again, it began to fall, as though in slow motion, floating, down, down, down toward her lap. Then up again, as high as her chest, then faltering, then down once more. From the lumpy blue chair across the room I watched her struggle, her swollen hand wrapped in a tensor bandage that was yet again coming loose. No matter that she'd waved me off. It was time to help.

But I remained on the edge of the plastic seat, urging her silently to finish what she'd started. Surely, she could still perform this simple task. If only she kept trying, and I kept believing.

NINETEEN

The Flaw She Slips Through

WE HAD ONE DAY WITH LOU BACK AT THE APARTMENT after she'd completed that brutal round of treatment. In my memory, those last hours we spent together in Vancouver remain all wound up in the tensor bandages we were continually repositioning around her puffed-up hands. She was groggy, phlegmy, swollen. But she was also cheerfully sporting her wig, and glad to be home. The morning we left she rode with us to the airport. We hugged by the car, in the drop-off zone. She wore an oversized shirt of Glen's. I looked in her face, I know I did. But what did I see in her eyes? What words did we speak? These details are lost to me now.

Back in Toronto two weeks later, I sat at my desk at the *T.O!*, hunched over a notebook, making a to-do list for the week. I felt foolish, composing this list. The calls I was beholden to make, the interviews to arrange and research to conduct, were trivial. I kept it up, though, telling myself it would be an insult to Louisa if I sat around waiting for her to die. Glen had called the night before. "Things aren't good," he'd said. "It's going to happen soon."

How do you move through the day knowing that, in a distant city, your closest friend may be on the verge of drawing, or has already taken, her last breath? This isn't a reality you can dwell on without cease, but as soon as you notice your mind has wandered, you stop short. Could your inattention have tipped the balance? Could it be the factor that lets her fall from this world, the flaw she slips through?

The office was uncharacteristically quiet, Adam and Spence subdued. Had I told them when I'd come in? I'd meant to. I must have. When my phone rang, I picked it up as though I were expecting no one remarkable, just some local source returning my call. But it was Lou's dad. He said, "Anita, we have some sad news."

He said this in his rising, cracking voice that often sounded happy and tearful at the same time. He said "sad," not "bad." It seemed an important distinction.

"We lost Louisa this morning."

"No," I blurted. "Not yet. Already?" Yet I'd known this was coming. I'd been warned. I pictured the words Lou's dad had spoken screwing into his face, squeezing his eyes into slits and folding his skin into red ridges over his forehead and nose. Each time he uttered them he would be deformed anew.

The next thing I knew, I was walking home, weaving between apartment blocks, over sparse spring grass and through rundown parkettes, then along the bridge crossing the Don Valley with Adam at my side. He was not talking politics or Regent Park or anything, just quietly leading the way. It was a forty-minute walk. I let him lead, though I knew exactly where I was going, exactly where I lived.

I imagined walking into the apartment I shared with Nicky, into the living room, turning slowly around, seeing the TV, the window, the coat rack, the stool, not knowing what to do. There were phone calls I'd be bound make: to my sister, my parents, our other friends. Every person Louisa and I had ever met deserved a call. How would I find all these people? Yet I must. And soon. It was incomprehensible that anyone could be out there doing whatever they normally did on a weekday morning, drinking coffee or jogging or filing documents or sitting in traffic or dismantling an engine, not knowing that she was gone.

Adam remained silent beside me as we turned north on the east side of the valley. Random questions tumbled through my mind. Was there food in the fridge? Did we have any coffee? What could we have done that we hadn't?

We were passing the Don Jail when it dawned on me that very likely I would someday turn thirty, then forty, and so on, while Louisa would not. What would happen as I got older and she remained twenty-two? What would stay with me? Who would I talk with the way she and I had together mulled the things of this world?

I didn't want anything to happen to me. At all. Ever again. Yet it already was. A cool, light breeze brushed my face. Warm sunshine bore down on the broad grey sidewalk, onto Adam and me. A streetcar screeched past, and I stared as I always did on my way home at the green land swooping into the valley through Riverdale Park. Louisa no longer existed but this did, I did, walking up the road on an April morning with another friend.

MORE THAN A DECADE AFTER LOUISA DIED, I WAS OUT WEST for a conference. Glen and I drove to the West Vancouver cemetery Lou's mom had carefully selected as her final "home." It was a vast green field, mountains in the distance. Daffodils and magnolias bloomed. There were no tombstones, only plaques set in the ground. Lovely and peaceful, but I yearned for weeping monuments, lichen-encrusted tombs, names staring out at me from weathered, crooked stones.

Years before, under a tall cedar near the plaque marking Louisa's buried ashes, Glen and I had solemnly planted a yellow rose bush. It hadn't survived, and had become instead proof of the impractical, willful optimism we'd all, to some extent, shared. A yellow rose? Seriously? What had we been thinking? Roses were a profound undertaking, even for real gardeners. But, whatever. Lou wouldn't have been able to keep that bush alive, either.

Glen was now a husband and father, embroiled in work and family life. It had been a long while since he'd made the trip here. He was dismayed by the state of Lou's plaque. It had lost its shine. "It's so dirty," he said, touching a finger to the dull, gold letters. I had a toothbrush in my backpack. He found a T-shirt in the trunk of his car (a roomy SUV, the trusty old Tercel long gone).

We collected a cup of water from a nearby spout and got to work, scrubbing. The hardened dirt between the letters was stubborn: we had to give it some muscle. I remembered that Louisa used to clean the bathtub when she was worried or upset. Scouring is satisfying, clarifying. When we were finished, Glen went to throw the T-shirt and toothbrush out in a nearby trash can. He called back, "They're going to think someone's living in the park." He laughed. Then he shook his head and said, "Forget it," in that apologetic way that Louisa had loved. I looked down at her freshly glossy name and smiled.

SO MUCH IS MISSING. WE SANG THE MESSAGES ON OUR answering machine. Created the Hot-woman Handshake. Found the door to the roof of our twenty-two-storey co-op and looked out on the city at night—we drank in the lights, the sense of a teeming humanity, the infinite. To kill time at the bus stop, we belted out songs by the Monkees. Or she'd flash her eyes and declare, "I…feel…a dance coming on!" Then she'd burst into a stomping, jumping, twirling, arm-flailing minute, like a windup toy set loose. She brought Diet Coke and lime to parties, surreptitiously, in a purse. She once drove the wrong way on a quiet, cul-de-sac round-about, around and around, gripping the wheel and muttering ferociously, "I'm such a rebel. I'm such a rebel."

Twenty-five years ago and counting, Louisa, my true, essential, always-there-for-everything friend, died. We were twenty-two. She didn't feel cheated. That she'd embraced this acceptance and found peace was a blessing; it lent her dignity, grace, a perceptible glow. It may have eased her suffering. And her serenity was a parting gift for those of us who loved her, one that, for me, still yields comfort. But she was wrong: she'd most certainly been cheated. In the course of history, even in the course of a single day on Earth, she was hardly alone in that. We're a species that perpetually seeks solace, not only for our own particular claims to anguish, but for this roiling rush of human calamity within which we make our way. Lou had hoped I'd find safe harbour with Ryan. I did, for a time. She was right to worry for me before she died. I've been learning ever since how to exist in her wake, compiling who I am all over again, without her by my side.

EPILOGUE

Memory in Imparfait

WHEN SUMMER ARRIVED AFTER THAT FIRST YEAR IN HIGH school, I had three goldfish left from my ill-conceived science experiment. Louisa offered to care for them when my family went on holiday. I brought her the bowl, the food, a little net, basic instructions. Then we piled in the station wagon and drove east to Cape Breton, to visit my grandparents.

Back home three weeks later, we tumbled bleary-eyed out of the car. I helped unload and ran inside to call Louisa.

"You'd better come over," she said.

When she opened the door to me a little while later, she blurted, "I'm sorry! I didn't mean it! It was an accident."

Here's the story as Louisa told it. As she spoke, she mimed the actions she was describing, moving between the offending sink and the counter where the last surviving goldfish, seemingly content, darted about its bowl.

I decided to clean the bowl. Give them some fresh water. I went to fill the sink.

I turned on the tap, and then the phone rang. I went to answer it, and when I came back, I turned the water off, grabbed the net and scooped a fish from the bowl. I plopped it in the sink and went back for the next fish. When I came to drop this fish in, the first one was sort of swimming funny. Sideways. Hmm. Could be goofing around in the sink, I thought—all that extra room! I lowered the second fish in, went and scooped up the third fish, and turned back to the sink. Now the first fish was floating on its back, and the second fish was swimming funny.

I put the third fish back in the bowl.

She grabbed my shoulders and gave me a look of agonized remorse. *Okay. You know how I can never remember with that tap which way is hot or cold? After I answered the phone, I should have checked the temperature. But I didn't. I didn't think.*

Anita, the water was too hot. I scalded your goldfish! I killed them.

Can you ever forgive me?

I gripped her shoulders in return. "Louisa. I'm not going to miss them. Three fish? You know how much they poo? I was tired of cleaning the bowl."

I carted home the round glass bowl, the container of food, the last goldfish in a baggie full of water, and Louisa's tale of remorse.

I PLACED THAT LAST GOLDFISH, THE ONE LOUISA *DIDN'T* boil alive, on the grey stone mantle over the fireplace. I have no idea how long it survived: at some point it swims right out of my memory. In its place wriggles the goldfish my younger brother won at the Appleby Mall fair one summer. He named it Calvin, after the boy in the comic strip, and it lived for, what? Seven, eight, nine years? Longer than any reasonable goldfish should. One winter it turned a sickly grey-white. I called a pet store. Was it ill? Could you doctor a goldfish? They told me fish can lose their pigment, it was probably fine.

My inner skeptic kicked in: perhaps it was never really a gold-fish at all, but some other species. Poached, illegally bred. Some kind of fairground scam. It swam on and on, swishing the plastic seaweeds and lettuces in its little aquarium. I nearly wrote here that Lou thought it was cute, even after it became ugly. But it's just as likely the ghastly thing freaked her out, or that she barely noticed it at all. I'd have to ask her to be sure—and obviously I can't. I remain mesmerized, at times frustrated or saddened, occasionally outraged, by the eternity tied to that *can't*.

My parents finally moved out of that house a few years back, forty-four years after settling there. They're in a condo now and I'm sure that, as I do, they miss the old fire-place. I can still see the fish circling in its clear glass bowl against a backdrop of wood panelling, amid a constantly rotating display of greeting cards signed extravagantly with "loves" and *X*s and *O*s. Once, many years after Louisa died, I asked my parents if I could interview them about her. I sat across from them with a notebook. I wanted to know if my memories of those early years of our friendship meshed with theirs. Was it true that they'd been wary of her at first, but had been quickly won over? "I don't remember any of that," my mother said. "I remember being grateful that you'd found a friend. That you weren't alone." She meant: alone in the wilds of adolescence. Now that I'm older, and a parent, too, I know what she meant. I'm relieved on my own behalf.

There's no guarantee that, had she lived, my friendship with Louisa would have continued to thrive. We might have settled on the same block in the same city, our kids running back and forth between our houses, the two of us haunting one another's porches in the evenings. But who knows? Our alliance might have hit bottom, given the chance. We might have lost the need, or the energy, required for intimacy. We might have disappointed one another, grown apart.

At midlife, I find myself losing my grip on that distinction between *passé composé* and *imparfait*. I remember the clarity I once intuited, with such confidence. I'm sure I coached Louisa more than once, during our joint study sessions. I do still know that to say, "In French class that morning, Louisa passed me a note," is not at all the same as, "In French class that morning, Louisa was passing me a note." In the second statement, the action might be interrupted in the next line by something *else* that happened—or was happening—in that time and place. Each feels like the start of a different story, an alternate way of entering the past.

When our teacher compared us to one-celled creatures, she was trying to jolt us awake. Ever since, I have carried with me a mental image of blind, wobbly amoebas floating in liquid, occasionally colliding with another, their membranes pressing, overlapping. Now, video streams of magnified amoebas can be watched online. What forces draw them this way or that, toward one fellow and not the other? Their bubbling movement and perpetual shape-shifting is hypnotic. What was it Louisa wrote? "You have more than contributed to my life. You have *been* my life."

As the years accumulate, as I bump into new friendships that mix and mingle inside me with those from the past, I resist the finality of *passé composé*. Rather, I lack faith in it. It's not that I don't accept what's real. Louisa was born. Louisa and I became friends. Louisa died. I carry on.

These are facts, as are the events that took place in between and that have taken place since. But grammar fails to account for memory and its workings, for the continual overlay of plotlines and half-written stories in the most modest of lives. Even definitive moments, incidents with a clear beginning and end, rewind and replay. Revisiting them becomes habitual. And the variations, with regards to detail, focus, light, speed, emotional force—well, I hardly know where to begin.

French class. Grade nine. Bizarre teacher. Itchy kilt. I opened my binder and gasped. Louisa turned around.

Author's Note

SEVERAL NAMES AND SOME DETAILS HAVE BEEN CHANGED to protect privacy.

Portions of this story have appeared in earlier forms, as follows: "Late-Night Snack" in *The New Quarterly* 147, Summer 2018; "Frostbite" in *Prairie Fire* 4.1, Spring 2019; "Everything's Fine" in *Hamilton Arts & Letters* 11.2, 2018–19; and "Confessions of a Eulogist," which first appeared in the Banff Centre anthology *Word Carving: The Craft of Literary Journalism*, and later in my own book, *The Mystery Shopping Cart: Essays on Poetry and Culture*. "How to Be Friends with a Redhead," published in *Maisonneuve* 22, Winter 2007, received a National Magazine Award honourable mention. I'm tremendously grateful to the editors and publishers of these publications.

The account of Louisa's meeting with the oncologist in the chapter titled "Undertow" is adapted from her own written account. Excerpts appearing here from her diary and journal entries, both written and audio, are her own words, quoted directly from these sources.

The epigraph is reprinted with permission from the estate of Bronwen Wallace. I'm grateful for the generosity of her estate, and for the fierce attention Wallace paid to friendship in her writing.

The writing of early drafts of this book was funded, in part, by grants from the Canada Council for the Arts and the Ottawa Arts Council, a support for which I'm extremely thankful.

I first began to shape the memories and anecdotes here during a continuing education writing class taught by Elizabeth Hay at the University of Ottawa in 1995. Hay's initial encouragement helped sustain me over two and a half decades of fitful revision and narrative detours. Further welcome guidance (and sustenance!) came from Isabel Huggan, through the Humber School for Writers; Moira Farr, through the Banff Centre for the Arts' Literary and Cultural Journalism program; and Joan Thomas, through the Banff Centre's now sadly discontinued Wired Writing program. These four accomplished, witty, wise, and generous authors have served as guiding lights and examples for me. (A big shout-out to Fred Stenson, who shepherded Wired with such remarkable warmth for so many years.)

My thanks to Carmine Starnino for believing in this book enough to comb through an early draft seeking a suitable excerpt, and for that subsequent gruelling edit for *Maisonneuve* all those years ago.

I offer abundant thanks to Dilys Leman, Una McDonnell, and Lesley Buxton, the "Blast it Out Sucky" crew who red-pencilled draft after draft of pieces of this manuscript over many years. You three blessedly unforgiving readers and writerly companions: my love for you all is bottomless.

For their friendship and for Important Discussions, literary and otherwise, I also thank John Barton, Yvonne Blomer,

Chris Carder, Rod Charles, Pauline Conley, Moira Dann, Alyse Frampton, Craig Hiebert, Steph Khoury, Chris Knight, and particularly my sister, Wendy Lahey. For her wisdom and her buoying friendship, I am indebted to Molly Peacock. For blessedly honest feedback, I thank Patricia Young, and for her saving, late-in-the-game editorial suggestions, I'm heartily grateful to Alice Zorn. I also extend deep thanks to Mark Sutcliffe for productive feedback on the earliest (toughest to slog through) versions of this book.

My editor, Janice Zawerbny, is a wonder in whose perceptive, keen-eyed path I am so lucky to have landed. Thank you, Janice. I joyfully bow down to Linda Pruessen for her surgically precise copy edit. To Dan Wells and the crew at Biblioasis: thank you for giving this story a home, and a way out into the world.

Louisa's family members and my own have been informed many times over the years that this book was "under construction," "getting there," et cetera. To all of you, I extend my heartfelt thanks for your forbearance. (I also apologize for any arrogant nonsense emanating from my adolescent self, as portrayed in these pages.) I especially thank Louisa's parents and brothers and her then-boyfriend Glen for their understanding, and for sharing documents and artifacts.

I thank my own parents for their astonishing, unconditional trust, a gift that cannot be measured.

I'm grateful to Monique Holmes for too many things to describe here, but ultimately for her enduring friendship— for being my touchstone.

And not at all least, I thank my husband, Tom Good, for his good-natured willingness to live with me and my ghosts, and for the easy, roomy companionship within which I was finally able to complete this work.

To Henry, our son, I wish the blessing and comfort of friendship.

Despite many years of ill-conceived efforts to that end, I have not told Louisa's story here, only *my* story of Louisa and our friendship, which remains to me a miraculous occurrence that rewrote my youth. The Louisa in these pages is the one I knew, the Louisa I marvelled over and loved, and she may seem strange to others who were close to her—you will all have your own Louisas, not-quite-known to me.